The Angelic Host

Investigating Angels in the Bible and Second Temple Literature

Karsten C. Wille

Greatness University Publishers
www.greatnessuniversity.co.uk

ISBN: 978-1-913164-11-9
ISBN-13: 978-1-913164-11-9

DEDICATION

I would like to dedicate this book to my mother who has
tirelessly supported me in all my endeavors.

TABLE OF CONTENTS

ACKNOWLEDGMENTS

I would like to thank all the Hebrew scholars who stepped out of their comfort zone to contextualize Jewish thought during the second temple period, thus enabling us to gain a glimpse of the world view the New Testament writers were exposed to.

PREFACE

This book is a study of the Heavenly Host. It is a systematic review of all key words that pertain to 'spiritual beings' and angels. The word 'angel', is mentioned over 270 times in scripture, but this does not include other spiritual beings that also have a part to play in the biblical text. Church tradition has led us to view all the 'host of heaven' with this common term, which is insufficient in gaining an understanding of this mesmerizing topic. The images we rely on have largely been driven by Greek mythology and artists' impressions of either little babies with wings or beautiful figures with long flowing golden hair, halos, harps and elaborate gowns.

A deep analysis of scripture, however, separates fact from fiction and informs us of the history and appearance of these elusive beings both in speech and deed. I will be focusing on many references concerning the heavenly bodies in scripture and second temple literature to gain an idea of context and how the ancients viewed the topic to approach the subject with a clean slate. There is a big yearning towards the supernatural, including a desire to uncover every knowledge that is hidden. This study seeks to unravel many of the mysteries associated with spiritual beings and to take a look at the classifications that have been so difficult to define. The discovery of the Dead Sea Scrolls have aided our understanding immensely; sources that were not available to our Christian forefathers, who at the time did the best they could with the primary materials they had available. The Dead Sea Scrolls also included second temple literature and the much-discussed book of Enoch, which is crucial to angelology.

The Host of Heaven does not just include the good guys, but the fallen ones too, who were originally part of a unified divine council under God. We will be looking at the 'Divine Council', the 'Cherubim and Seraphim', 'The Angel of the Lord', 'Michael and Gabriel', 'The Adversary', 'Demons' and all characters pertaining to the hidden spiritual realm.

Names form the key to understanding the role of spiritual beings, so these will be looked at in detail to unlock our understanding of these characters. There are many books written about angels. Some books rely very heavily on just spiritual experience and little scripture. Others, are very biblically based, but are difficult to grasp as they read very much like a grammar book, delving heavily into the Old Testament Hebrew and New Testament Greek, accompanied by more footnotes than decipherable content. I have written this piece in view of presenting the findings as simply as possible with a broad sweep of scripture, second temple literature and historical sources. This includes key learning points from each chapter and a summary of the findings of this study to allow the reader to come away with a full understanding of the topic in context. None of the ideas presented in this book are originally my own, rather form the world view of the second temple period and the early church, firmly grounded in the teachings of Irenaeus. This material is recommended for Christians who are mature in the faith.

ELOHIM

When we begin our Biblical journey, the first thing we consider is the continued story that unfolds between man and God. There is, however, a whole array of characters portrayed in scripture that aid our understanding of the spirit realm including Angels and Demons. They are cast as spiritual beings that inhabit the realm of the heavens, overlapping with our earthly dimension. These spiritual beings have their own characteristics and the authors of the Bible used specific key words to define all the inhabitants of the spiritual realm. Old Testament Hebrew uses the word: 'Elohim', whereas the New Testament Greek uses the word: 'Theos'. The difficulty in gaining an overall picture is assessing which word is being referred to. This depends on the use of capital letters and context, which requires someone in the know how to determine who is being referred to in the spiritual realm, whether 'God', or another spiritual being. 'Elohim', is therefore not a specific name, but a title. In the same way a parent may have a lot of different names and abbreviations for different kinds of people: it still refers to the same role in the family the parental figure possesses. In the same way as a mark of respect I may call someone 'sir', and could be referring to a larger group of people who serve that same function. A big term of respect in Hebrew was the term 'Yahweh', for God, being the name revealed to Moses. Titles, however, also included the key word 'Elohim', which was defined as a category, with full knowledge of who they were referring to. Of course it is evident that God was in a league of his own, which is why you would see Yahweh referred to as 'Elohim of Elohim', emphasizing that he was above all others. They would also differentiate this category by saying that: 'There is no Elohim beside Yahweh', indicating that there was none by comparison as he was seen as Creator God (1 Kings 8:23)(Exodus 15:11) (Deuteronomy 3:24)(Psalm 97:9). Christianity and Judaism are of course Monotheistic Religions. Therefore, the Biblical writers are clear in their communication, that there is only one spiritual being out there who is the Prime Mover and Creator of all things including the key term 'Elohim'. This is at the exclusion of other spiritual rulers with the same title. Monotheism found in scripture communicates that one specific Elohim 'Yahweh', is above all other elohim, meaning other spiritual beings in the heavenly realm. Elohim in scripture is a term used as either 'God', or other 'spiritual beings'.

There are a number of elohim in scripture that have a number of titles including 'Host of Heaven', 'Sons of God', 'Holy Ones', 'Heavenly Ones', and 'Divine Council' (Heiser, 2015). We will be exploring these terms in greater depth in the next chapters.

Learning Points

- *Yahweh Elohim is God.*
- *Elohim can also mean 'other spiritual beings'.*

THE DIVINE COUNCIL

If we historically look at all cultures of the past, there is no escaping the fact that wherever one finds oneself in the world, there is a belief in the spiritual realm, mirroring the life in the natural. This is of course the same in Judeo-Christian thinking, not just a process resembling, but also overlapping realms. Scripture highlights the difference of earthly with divine, by defining God's space as the sky or heavens, as what is seen above can be viewed as timeless and eternal. We may see the stars as simple luminaries, but the authors of the Bible likened them to spiritual beings and used the mystery behind them to communicate their nature. Scripture calls them 'The Sons of God', 'Rulers and Authorities', and in certain instances 'The Divine Council'. The study of these terms and application to theology have been largely overlooked in applied Christian thinking. We see the introduction to the 'Divine Council' in the first book of Genesis when they are referred to as 'Hosts of Heaven'. The sun, moon and stars. Here they are seen as signs of power and stature, signs pointing to the ultimate status in the universe and God's omnipotence. They are appointed to rule over the day and night. They celebrated with joy when God used his unlimited creativity to create the world.

'when the morning stars sang together and all the **sons of God** *shouted for joy'?* **Job 38:7**

Christian theology has largely ignored the existence of other spiritual beings in the heavenlies and we have always used a general term of 'angel', being a 'messenger' accomplishing a divine mission or relaying an important message. Could it be, however, that there are indeed other spiritual beings in conversation with God, joining in the decision making on earth like a spiritual staff team? This is not a reflection on God's omniscience, neither his omnipotence, but he clearly enjoys sharing decision-making with the 'heavenly host'. There are instances in scripture where God invites the 'Divine Council' to participate in the making of decisions on earthly matters. One of these instances is when they decided how the ungodly Jewish King Ahab was to be brought down:

'And the LORD *said, 'Who will entice Ahab, that he may go up and fall at Ramoth-gilead?' And one said one thing, and another said another.* ^{21} *Then a spirit came forward and stood before the* LORD, *saying, 'I will entice him.'* ^{22} *And the* LORD *said to him, 'By what means?' And he said, 'I will go out, and will be a lying spirit in the mouth of all his prophets.' And he said, 'You are to entice him, and you shall succeed; go out and do so.'*
2 Kings 22: 20-22

Another example is in the book of Job when God has discussions with the Divine Council 'Sons of God', based on rewarding those who do good. This epic account unfolds, as the adversary (a former member of the Divine Council) questioned God's omniscience. This was something God was perfectly willing to defend with a whole array of divine assembly watching the events unfold on earth. In the last chapter God is proven right for putting his trust in Job. The book of Job next to Genesis is considered to be one of the oldest books of the Bible.

⁶'Now there was a day when the **sons of God** *came to present themselves before the* LORD, *and Satan also came among them.* ⁷*The* LORD *said to Satan, "From where have you come?" Satan answered the* LORD *and said, "From going to and fro on the earth, and from walking up and down on it."* ⁸*And the* LORD *said to Satan, "Have you considered my servant Job, that there is none like him on the earth, a blameless and upright man, who fears God and turns away from evil?"* ⁹*Then Satan answered the* LORD *and said, "Does Job fear God for no reason?* ¹⁰*Have you not put a hedge around him and his house and all that he has, on every side? You have blessed the work of his hands, and his possessions have increased in the land.* ¹¹*But stretch out your hand and touch all that he has, and he will curse you to your face."* ¹²*And the* LORD *said to Satan, "Behold, all that he has is in your hand. Only against him do not stretch out your hand." So Satan went out from the presence of the* LORD'. **Job 1:6-22**

It is clear by the very nature of the titles that meetings take place in a heavenly council with the exchange of suggestions and ideas and an ultimate decision taking place to grant permission for a certain method of approach. It isn't that God requires help to come to a decision about anything, but he seems to enjoy the involvement of his heavenly members of the council, thereby giving responsibility and authority to other spiritual beings. Not so much the influence of those titled 'Sons of God' though, and I will elaborate on this further when we explore how some of these spiritual beings went rogue. We can also see God's desire for shared rule in the Garden of Eden, when God gives Adam responsibility to subdue the earth and look after it, but as with some of the Angelic Host, man rebelled and did what was right in his own eyes in a fallen state.

The building of Babylon was a prime example of man's rebellion towards God's command to disperse and to be fruitful and multiply. Man built a tower called 'Babel' as an idol of worship to themselves and other spiritual beings. Babel was an elevated platform where humans worshipped a deity. This was the origin of Babylon (Babel). When Moses and Isaiah recalled the origin of this city and tower, they saw more than just man revolting repeatedly against God's commands, but they also saw a spiritual rebellion among the 'heavenly host'. This spiritual rebellion can be characterized as members of the 'Divine Council' who didn't want to submit to the throne room of God, neither represent Him in His Kingdom matters, but wanted their own autonomy. They wanted to be just like God, so they rebelled. This characterizes the third fall. They did this by convincing humans to worship them instead of the Elohim of Elohim. These created beings thus took the place of God on elevated platforms. The existence of Babylon and the apocalyptic metaphor of the name thus becomes the combined image of rebellion towards God in the heavens and on the earth. After God confuses the language of the people, building stops and God topples the tower. He scatters them to the corners of the earth and then came the formation of Nations.

The Book of Deuteronomy is key in communicating how God scattered the former members of the divine council with the humans to the same set locations.

'Remember the days of old; consider the years of many generations; ask your father, and he will show you, your elders, and they will tell you.
⁸ When the Most High gave to the nations their inheritance, when he divided mankind, he fixed the borders⌟ of the peoples according to the number of the **sons of God'.** *Deuteronomy 32:7-8*

The nations were thus divided unto spiritual rulers as leaders of geographic locations. The chaos, injustices and overall corruption that is observed in these accounts of those nations are highlighted by the Biblical authors as a two dimensional phenomenon. Not just a physical one, but also a spiritual realm that is part and parcel of these deeds with shared responsibility. These spiritual entities wanted to be worshipped as idols in the form of debauchery, money and displays of might. Very much like the world we see today, when those in authority give themselves over to the flesh and the spiritual beings that hide behind the idols worshipped: thus chaos manifests itself.

A good example of this principle in operation is the account of Moses and the Israelites as they exit Egypt and God punishes 10 of the gods belonging to the biggest superpower at the time. Initially the death of all the Hebrew boys were not just orchestrated by Pharaoh himself, but also inspired by the gods of Egypt.

*12 'For I will pass through the land of Egypt that night, and I will strike all the firstborn in the land of Egypt, both man and beast; and on **all the gods of Egypt I will execute judgments:** I am the* LORD. *13 The blood shall be a sign for you, on the houses where you are. And when I see the blood, I will pass over you, and no plague will befall you to destroy you, when I strike the land of Egypt'.* **Exodus 12:12-13**

This prompted God to bring Egypt to justice, including Pharaoh and his gods. Each plague God released upon the Egyptians was a god the Egyptians worshipped. It was not just a slap in the face to their worship of these entities but a never-ending reminder in history that Yahweh is the God of all and that there is none beside him. It was in this process of the rule of these gods being destroyed that God takes a remnant of humanity again and calls them his own. He introduces a third covenant with man through the leadership of Moses and puts in motion another way to view the world and behave. As of course with the Noahide covenant and the Abrahamic covenant, man even under the leadership of Moses lacks the moral responsibility to uphold the covenant with God and they return to the gods of Egypt, Babylon and other entities.

The Hebrews return to slavery being dragged off and exiled in Babylon. They become subjects again to another nation and the spiritual rulers and entities overseeing this empire. They await patiently under many trials and persecutions, their long-awaited return to the promised land.

It is in the land of Israel that we are introduced to Jesus. The very incarnation of God who lived amongst us as a man. Jesus was here to save the world and take it back from these rebels. Here again we see this duality of human and spiritual rebels at work, putting their plans in place in unison. Jesus addresses this concept as one and the same, not merely human rebellion and disobedience. We see the plot unfold in an overlapping of the natural and spiritual realm. When Jesus arrived in Jerusalem on Palm Sunday (Passover) he was announcing this very fact that, all the prophecies of the Old Testament were coming to pass and that spiritual authorities were being disarmed in a display of both ultimate strength and meekness. The largest exodus was about to take place, freeing humanity from the control of the spiritual rulers of darkness. This was accomplished by his sin offering on the cross, God, giving himself as a ransom for many.

[45] *'For even the Son of Man came not to be served but to serve, and to give his life as a ransom for many."* **Mark 10:45**

Jesus defeated the powers of darkness, by allowing them a grim time of complete control as they unleashed their hate, violence and verbal poison. For the purpose of the whole of humanity Jesus countered this grim appearance of a battle initially seen as lost with the strength of his love and the power of his resurrection life. Following this event he was able to announce to his own that all power and authority had been given to him. Through the process of the incarnation (putting on flesh), God was the ultimate human and divine partner. This was indeed what the Gospel was all about. The good news and power unto salvation. This is why the disciples shared their faith to a people who understood more fully this duality between humanity and the divine and that indeed Jesus was the risen Christ (ultimate spiritual being) whom they should follow. This person who showed himself in the flesh and who was truly divine would also model a way to be truly human and provide the example of how to practise spirituality in the true essence of freedom.

The victory won by Jesus indeed disarmed them. The apostle Paul writes:

15 He disarmed the rulers and authorities[a] and put them to open shame, by triumphing over them in him. **Colossians 2:15**

They were, however, not completely done away with. These spiritual forces still exist and cause just as much trouble as they ever did before, just not with a legal right over humanity. They are the root cause of a corrupt world. This is why we are required to love our neighbor and be forgiving to those who persecute us and mistreat us. Our enemy is therefore not other humans, but the spiritual entities that seek to destroy us. These spiritual authorities don't just stand behind idols of wood, stone and iron, but inhabit the very cultural idols we have that inspire one man to war against another, whether in reasoning, or outright division and violence. So if we are perceptive in recognizing this age old account of history repeating itself again and again, we recognize the fallen element of the 'Divine Council' at work, perpetuating the rebellion they started at the beginning of the age. This enemy is old, wise, calculated and has developed its strategies over the years, fine-tuning them to the weaknesses of man. This is why the Apostle Paul tells us to put on the full armor of God:

10 'Finally, be strong in the Lord and in the strength of his might. 11 Put on the whole armor of God, that you may be able to stand against the schemes of the devil. 12 For we do not wrestle against flesh and blood, but against the rulers, against the authorities, against the cosmic powers over this present darkness, against the spiritual forces of evil in the heavenly places. 13 Therefore take up the whole armor of God, that you may be able to withstand in the evil day, and having done all, to stand firm. 14 Stand therefore, having fastened on the belt of truth, and having put on the breastplate of righteousness, [15] and, as shoes for your feet, having put on the readiness given by the gospel of peace. [16] In all circumstances take up the shield of faith, with which you can extinguish all the flaming darts of the evil one; [17] and take the helmet of salvation, and the sword of the Spirit, which is the word of God, [18] praying at all times in the Spirit, with all prayer and supplication. To that end, keep alert with all perseverance, making supplication for all the saints, [19] and also for me, that words may be given to me in opening my mouth boldly to proclaim the mystery of the gospel, [20] for which I am an ambassador in chains, that I may declare it boldly, as I ought to speak. **Ephesians 6:10-20**

The character traits of Jesus are present in the armor of God and are key in defeating the enemy. Faithfulness, justice and peace. Our primary weapon in defeating the adversary is the sword of the Spirit, the Word of God. This is the truly inspired account of Jesus defeating the rebel powers of darkness with the divine power of his love.

Learning Points

- *Angel means 'messenger' (malach). It is a description of a particular function.*
- *Angels can be embodied and manifest in physical form, or influence events on earth in disembodied form as spirits (2 Kings 22:2-23)*
- *Terms used for spiritual beings can also be 'Sons of God', 'Rulers and Authorities', 'Holy Ones', 'Heavenly Ones', 'Host of Heaven', 'Principalities and Powers', 'Divine Council'.*
- *There are angels of God, and angels that rebelled and remain in a fallen state. (Some former members of the Divine Council).*
- *The spiritual realm overlaps with the natural realm.*
- *The ten plagues were a judgement not just on the people of Egypt, but on the Gods of Egypt as well. (Exodus 12:12-13)*
- *In the New Testament, Jesus was/is the ultimate spiritual being.*
- *Jesus disarmed all spiritual authorities. (Col 2:15)*

ANGELS, CHERUBIM & SERAPHIM

Continuing our theme of spiritual entities, we have seen that the 'Divine Council' are individuals who are or some at least were on God's board meetings and either current or former members of the 'Heavenly Host'. In scripture there is much to suggest that one term is not sufficient. When looking at spiritual beings, the key word 'angel', is simply too simplistic, as we also have other spiritual beings including cherubim and seraphim. Systematically reviewing scripture and looking at the terms referring to the 'heavenly host' merely as 'angels', gives us a very incomplete picture. This is a term used to classify most things in the unseen realm, but this does not foster the understanding Hebrews would have had about the spiritual world. A lot of the important vocabulary linked to linguistics was lost over time and gentiles were generally ignorant of the Old Testament theologies regarding the 'Heavenly Host'.

The term 'angel', comes from the Hebrew word 'mal'ak', meaning 'messenger'. Humans can also have that job description sending messages back and forth (Gen 32:3, 7; Deut 2:26; Neh 6:3; 2 Samuel 11:9). This is a term that describes function, whether a spiritual being or not. Dr. Heiser points out, that the terms that describe function can be attributed to 'Angel', 'Minister', 'Watcher', 'Host', 'Mediator', 'Cherubim', 'Seraphim'. These terms serve as job descriptions or attributes relating to some task (Heiser 2018).

There are many functions of the 'Heavenly Host', some of which are attributed to Cherubim. There are, however, so many misconceptions about this term. How many times have you seen a cute chubby kid being called a little cherub? And why might one ask? Well this is where the mythology comes in. For centuries for the purpose of the study of angelology we have relied on Greek Mythology present in our religious paintings, mosaics, tapestries and stain glass windows. No theologians complained when artists would link Christianity and terms found in it to the cultural myths and appearances of spiritual beings recorded by the ancients in Greek legends. A Cherub is not a fat baby with wings preparing to shoot an arrow at someone to ignite love on Valentine's Day. This is the imagery we need to start moving away from. Cherubim are daunting and imposing figures to whom one would generally not attribute the word 'cute'. If we look at scripture, we see them described as a number of creatures in one, almost in the form of a hybrid spiritual being. Their appearance is never constant and they shift physical traits depending on which account we read. They stand guard between the spiritual and natural realm guarding heaven. If you were to come across a Cherub, you would know that you are about to enter the presence of the Most High. The first time we see Cherubim, is when they are guarding the entrance to the Garden of Eden following the fall of man.

*24 He drove out the man, and at the east of the garden of Eden he placed the **cherubim** and a flaming sword that turned every way to guard the way to the tree of life.* **Genesis 3:24**

The Garden of Eden was sacred space, considered to be Holy, a place where the now disobedient Adam and Eve are no longer welcome to enter. Adam and Eve are banned from this space, because they cannot be trusted. God gave them one commandment and they broke it. The one commandment was so easy to keep, therefore the punishment was so difficult to bear, in the form of complete exclusion from this sacred space.

The Biblical account is, however, not a prolonged exclusion, but God inviting man to be part of fellowship with him again. This is why he gave the Israelites a miniature version of Eden to carry around with them in the wilderness in the form of the 'Tabernacle', followed by a fixed dwelling place for God on the Temple Mount in Jerusalem. This is significant as in both the sacred space of the 'Tabernacle', and 'Temple', we see the appearance of Cherubim engraved and formed as statues. This served as a reminder to those officiating at the altar that they were indeed in the presence of God. Cherubim are thus always in connection with sacred space. Once a year the High Priest after all the cleansing procedures would enter a place in the Temple called the 'Holy of Holies'. There he would come across this sacred box called the 'Arc of the Covenant'. Formed in one piece upon the box were two golden Cherubim. This formed the footstool of God's thrown, which the Cherubim were carrying. Psalm 99 writes;

*'God sits enthroned above the **Cherubim***'.

The throne was clearly not in view, just the box which was God's footstool referred to as the 'Arc of the Covenant'. The reason why there was no representation of a throne, was because God was never supposed to be represented in any type of physical image. You would not have had this in the temple, neither will you see this in any orthodox synagogues today.

The Throne of God, however, only became visible, when the prophets had visions of God sitting on his throne. There has been much debate as to the physical representation of these spiritual beings to whether scripture is an anatomy lesson as to their physical attributes in literalism, or if the appearance of the cherubim in the visions were meant to be metaphorical to aid the understanding of the human beholding the scene. Isaiah's vision of the throne of God and the Cherubim guarding its sacred space represents these beings in a number of forms promoting the majesty and glory of God's creation. To add to the confusion of classifications of heavenly beings, here they are referred to as Seraphim and scripturally speaking, in role and function, there is very little to tell them apart. An interesting point to note is that the term 'Seraphim' actually means 'snake' in Hebrew. A matter of fact, most scholars believe Cherubim and Seraphim are one and the same type of spiritual beings (Sproul 2011). Isaiah 6:1-7

6 In the year that King Uzziah died I saw the Lord sitting upon a throne, high and lifted up; and the train' of his robe filled the temple. ²Above him stood the seraphim. Each had six wings: with two he covered his face, and with two he covered his feet, and with two he flew. ³And one called to another and said:

"Holy, holy, holy is the LORD of hosts;
the whole earth is full of his glory!"

⁴And the foundations of the thresholds shook at the voice of him who called, and the house was filled with smoke. ⁵And I said: "Woe is me! For I am lost; for I am a man of unclean lips, and I dwell in the midst of a people of unclean lips; for my eyes have seen the King, the LORD of hosts!"

⁶Then one of the seraphim flew to me, having in his hand a burning coal that he had taken with tongs from the altar. ⁷And he touched my mouth and said: "Behold, this has touched your lips; your guilt is taken away, and your sin atoned for."

We see in these verses that the seraphim are almost forming a heavenly choir giving praise to their maker. The representation of these animal figures (especially cherubim) with wings are a manifestation of creatures with strength. Bulls, lions and eagles, so even their presence alone lets one know that one is in the presence of might, power and majesty. Technically, these are not really angels. They are 'throne guardians' and as mentioned before, guard sacred space to prevent the defilement of anything or anyone unholy. God's glory and holiness is thus worth protecting. The burning coal placed upon Isaiah's lips by the seraphim was a cleansing procedure performed as an act of guarding God's holiness. In the case of the ancient superpower of Egypt, it was the seraphim (cobras) that were used as the throne guardians, protecting the majesty of the Pharaoh. There is no example of either cherubim or seraphim appearing to man on earth to deliver a message (malach) or to assist humans on earth with a task. They are purely spiritual beings that guard sacred space.

This leads us back to angels. We do see scripture referring to cherubim and seraphim with wings, but angels we do not. Angels are messengers of God that work on His behalf and their purpose is to minister to those on earth (malach). If we address the issue of the mythology of angels, we do not have any evidence biblically that they have wings. A matter of fact, they look like us. More daunting of course if need be, but generally they blend in quite nicely. As humans we do not have physical access to the throne room of God, so God uses these messengers to reach out to us, as 'messenger', is what the key word 'angel' means. We see a number of events when angels appear to key characters in scripture, for example the annunciation (announcing the soon coming birth of Christ to Mary).

26 In the sixth month the angel Gabriel was sent from God to a city of Galilee named Nazareth, 27 to a virgin betrothed[a] to a man whose name was Joseph, of the house of David. And the virgin's name was Mary. 28 And he came to her and said, "Greetings, O favored one, the Lord is with you!"[b] 29 But she was greatly troubled at the saying, and tried to discern what sort of greeting this might be. 30 And the angel said to her, "Do not be afraid, Mary, for you have found favor with

God. ³¹ *And behold, you will conceive in your womb and bear a son, and you shall call his name Jesus.* ³² *He will be great and will be called the Son of the Most High. And the Lord God will give to him the throne of his father David,* ³³ *and he will reign over the house of Jacob forever, and of his kingdom there will be no end."* **Luke 1:26-33**

The job description of angels is not merely delivering messages to the people of God, but also to accomplish missions. An example of an angel intervening in the natural realm is when Peter was released from prison:

⁶ *Now when Herod was about to bring him out, on that very night, Peter was sleeping between two soldiers, bound with two chains, and sentries before the door were guarding the prison.* ⁷ *And behold, an angel of the Lord stood next to him, and a light shone in the cell. He struck Peter on the side and woke him, saying, "Get up quickly." And the chains fell off his hands.* ⁸ *And the angel said to him, "Dress yourself and put on your sandals." And he did so. And he said to him, "Wrap your cloak around you and follow me."* ⁹ *And he went out and followed him. He did not know that what was being done by the angel was real, but thought he was seeing a vision.* ¹⁰ *When they had passed the first and the second guard, they came to the iron gate leading into the city. It opened for them of its own accord, and they went out and went along one street, and immediately the angel left him.* ¹¹ *When Peter came to himself, he said, "Now I am sure that the Lord has sent his angel and rescued me from the hand of Herod and from all that the Jewish people were expecting." Acts 12:6-11*

Of course, in angelology one can see a clear ranking system of archangel and angel. You have very powerful angels like Gabriel meaning 'God is my power', and Michael 'Who is like God?'. The important learning point as to prevent any kind of worship of these heavenly hosts is the meaning of their names themselves. Both Gabriel's name and the name of Michael do not point to the majesty of the spiritual being, but to the glory of God himself. As humans who are created in the image and likeness of God, angels are thus images of both his presence and his power (Mackie 2019). This is how the 'Sons of God', fell as reported in Deuteronomy, because these overseers sought glory for themselves, thereby, sentencing their lives to everlasting separation from God. Yahweh does not provide a process of redemption for rebellious members of his 'Heavenly Host'.

The whole topic of angels is of course very fascinating, but also comes with a strong warning. We are not encouraged to look for them. If they have a mission or are given a message for the people of God, they find us. Needless to say, the supportive role they play is to re-establish the Kingdom of God on earth and to help fulfill God's plan. Angels are therefore used to show the way and serve the people of God. Most of the time, one isn't even going to know about their presence, neither their supernatural intervention in the natural realm.

Learning Points

- *There are many functions of the heavenly host.*
- *Cherubim are daunting and imposing figures appearing in scripture as human/animal hybrid spiritual beings.*
- *Cherubim shift traits according to different Biblical accounts.*
- *Cherubim stand guard between the spiritual and natural realm guarding heaven.*
- *Cherubim and Seraphim are throne guardians that guard sacred space.*
- *We only have one Biblical account of Seraphim.*
- *Seraphim form a heavenly choir in the throne room and guard the holiness of God.*
- *Seraph can also mean 'serpent,' or 'burning ones'.*
- *Cherubim are always portrayed as creatures of majesty and strength with faces of bulls, lions and eagles.*
- *Cherubim and Seraphim are not angels and do not peform functions on earth to deliver messages (malach), or intervene in human affairs.*
- *Cherubim and Seraphim do have wings.*

- *Cherubim, Seraphim and the archangel Michael are images of God's presence and power.*

THE ANGEL OF THE LORD

As previously explored we discovered there are two overlapping realms. The natural and the spiritual, recognizing the difference between the heavens and the earth, both active in each other. To make things simpler it can be defined as the space we inhabit and the space spiritual beings inhabit. Our realm seems to be pretty standard: however, sometimes the heavenly realm can manifest itself on earth with this overlap. This is evident in many accounts in scripture. When heaven manifests itself on earth, we have the appearance of someone completely amazing: 'The Angel of the Lord'. We have had a brief introduction to angels, who are messengers from God performing assigned missions, but the 'Angel of the Lord', is clearly no low level elohim or spiritual being. When we have reference to 'the Angel of the Lord', we are forced to think deeper as to the full nature of the entity at hand, as the personal pronouns communicate far more than the appearance of an angel, but rather Yahweh himself. Initially one may think that a mere angel (as a messenger) is conveying a message in the earthly realm, but upon closer inspection, it is difficult to distinguish between the two possibilities. This topic has been widely debated over the centuries. One of these examples is in the Book of Genesis when we have the account of Hagar, the Egyptian servant who runs away.

⁶ But Abram said to Sarai, "Behold, your servant is in your power; do to her as you please." Then Sarai dealt harshly with her, and she fled from her.

⁷ The angel of the LORD found her by a spring of water in the wilderness, the spring on the way to Shur. ⁸ And he said, "Hagar, servant of Sarai, where have you come from and where are you going?" She said, "I am fleeing from my mistress Sarai." ⁹ The angel of the LORD said to her, "Return to your mistress and submit to her." ¹⁰ The angel of the LORD also said to her, "I will surely multiply your offspring so that they cannot be numbered for multitude." ¹¹ And the angel of the LORD said to her,

"Behold, you are pregnant
and shall bear a son.
You shall call his name Ishmael,[l]
because the LORD has listened to your affliction.
¹² He shall be a wild donkey of a man,
his hand against everyone
and everyone's hand against him,
and he shall dwell over against all his kinsmen."

¹³ So she called the name of the LORD who spoke to her, "You are a God of seeing,"[d] for she said, "Truly here I have seen him who looks after me."[l] ¹⁴ Therefore the well was called Beer-lahai-roi;[l] it lies between Kadesh and Bered.

¹⁵ And Hagar bore Abram a son, and Abram called the name of his son, whom Hagar bore, Ishmael. ¹⁶ Abram was eighty-six years old when Hagar bore Ishmael to Abram. **Genesis 16:6-16**

The Angel of Yahweh is calling to Hagar, but then equally the language moves on to personal pronouns , 'I will multiply your offspring'. Hagar's response is also very telling as she exclaims 'You are the God of the seeing'. The only conclusion we can make from this example is that the 'Angel of the Lord' is clearly Yahweh. This can indeed be puzzling, as scripture is clear that you cannot look upon God and live. The crossing over between 'Angel of the Lord' and 'Yahweh', communicates an oxymoron, or perhaps more aptly put, some type of dualism. God is indeed not within our realm of grasp, but this does not mean that he doesn't reveal himself to mankind in ways that foster understanding in the physical realm. The 'Angel of the Lord' is thus a description in the Bible whereby Yahweh himself intervenes in the world and becomes visible to common man. He is therefore Yahweh, but separate from Yahweh manifesting himself to us. Throughout the Bible we see glimpses of sacred space experienced in visions by Daniel, Ezekiel and Isaiah. These prophets all see and experience an unimaginable person, full of power and glory who sits on a throne called Yahweh. This is indeed the same person as manifest in the world referred to as 'Angel of the Lord'. The Bible communicates this theology quite clearly in the account of Moses and the Burning Bush. Exodus 3:1-4:

*3 Now Moses was tending the flock of Jethro his father-in-law, the priest of Midian, and he led the flock to the far side of the wilderness and came to Horeb, the mountain of God. ² There the **angel of the LORD** appeared to him in flames of fire from within a bush. Moses saw that though the bush was on fire it did not burn up. ³ So Moses thought, "I will go over and see this strange sight—why the bush does not burn up."*

*⁴ When **the LORD** saw that he had gone over to look, **God** called to him from within the bush, "Moses! Moses!"*

And Moses said, "Here I am." **Exodus 3:1-4**

This mysterious figure is at first referred to as 'The Angel of the Lord', then, 'The Lord' and lastly 'God'. Further down the line after the Exodus has taken place, Moses discovers that the person originally in the burning bush is the same individual leading them out into the wilderness in the form of a cloud by day and a pillar of fire by night. This is the same almighty entity who resides in the tabernacle that travelled with them and later on the temple that stood in Jerusalem. The tabernacle formed sacred space as a literal throne room for God. The Angel of the Lord is the Holy personage of God appearing in many respects like a human. It is quite clear where we can be going from here, when equating God and man together as one, as this points toward Jesus and the incarnation. This is made very clear to us in the 1st Chapter of John's Gospel as we are told that Jesus existed for all eternity and that He was with God and was God:

*1 'In the beginning was the Word, and the Word was with God, and the Word was God. ² He was with God in the beginning. ³ Through him all things were made; without him nothing was made that has been made. ⁴ In him was life, and that life was the light of all mankind. ⁵ The light shines in the darkness, and the darkness has not overcome it'. **John 1:1-5***

The incarnation shows us the perfect example that Jesus was distinct from God, but also was God. This in itself was a similar anomaly we discovered between the 'Angel of the Lord' and 'Yahweh'. Further on in chapter 1 we see very much the same pattern, in that He made his dwelling among us:

*¹⁴ 'The Word became flesh and made his dwelling among us. We have seen his glory, the glory of the one and only Son, who came from the Father, full of grace and truth'. **John 1:14***

This was the same presence of the God in the Temple living amongst man. Jesus kept His Glory hidden from man and showed His divine nature only through miracles. An exception to this rule, was when He gave them a glimpse of his true personage during the transfiguration:

17 'After six days Jesus took with him Peter, James and John the brother of James, and led them up a high mountain by themselves. ² There he was transfigured before them. His face shone like the sun, and his clothes became as white as the light. ³ Just then there appeared before them Moses and Elijah, talking with Jesus'. **Matthew 17:1-3**

The Old Testament shows us 'The Angel of the Lord', who appears to a certain extent like a man and the New Testament through the incarnation shows Jesus as fully God and fully man. The title of 'Angel of the Lord', is not used in the New Testament. This was done to avoid the notion or conception that Jesus was limited to an angel, not allowing any chance of downgrading his divinity. To the writers of the New Testament it was evident that Jesus was Yahweh, fully manifested in the flesh, to fulfil the mission of reconciling man to God, forever reuniting both the realms of heaven and earth.

A matter of fact, for centuries the scribes and teachers of the law were trying to figure out who this mysterious figure was, as scripture presented the problem of the possibility of some kind of dualism between two Yahwehs. One as Yahweh in all His Glory and the other manifest as a man in the natural realm. Who was this second figure they asked? This was brought to an abrupt realisation when Jesus stood before Caiaphas the priest. The term 'son of man', was the term Jesus frequently used. He used it again in Matthew 26, thus claiming that He was that person whom the teachers of the law knew would put Jesus in the position of the Most High. When Jesus quoted Daniel 7, it sealed the deal:

*⁶⁴ Jesus *said to him, "You have said it yourself. But I tell you, from now on you will see the **Son of Man** sitting at the right hand of power, and coming on the clouds of heaven."*

⁶⁵ Then the high priest tore his ⁽ᴵ⁾ robes and said, "He has blasphemed! What further need do we have of witnesses? See, you have now heard the blasphemy; ⁶⁶ what do you think?" They answered, "He deserves death!" **Matthew 26:64-66**

Caiaphas the priest thus condemned Jesus to death, when Jesus quoted Daniel 7:13-14 about Himself, as this was the final straw they needed to prove that he was calling himself God. This is the scripture Jesus was quoting from:

13 "I saw in the night visions,

and behold, with the clouds of heaven
*there came one **like a son of man**,*
and he came to the Ancient of Days
and was presented before him.
14 And to him was given dominion
and glory and a kingdom,
that all peoples, nations, and languages
should serve him;
his dominion is an everlasting dominion,
which shall not pass away,
and his kingdom one
that shall not be destroyed".

Daniel 7:13-14

It was this human presentation of God the ancients struggled with, however, through the Old Testament term 'Angel of the Lord': furthermore, Jesus referring to Himself as 'The Son of Man', He was able to reveal himself verbally to those who knew and understood scripture. It was the teachers of the law He accused of blaspheming the Holy Spirit, as they were the ones who should have known better and wilfully engaged in apostasy rejecting 'The Son of Man'. In conclusion it is clear who the 'Angel of the Lord' is: The 'Angel of the Lord', is Jesus.

Learning Points

-   The *'Angel of the Lord'*, is a description in the Bible whereby Yahweh himself intervenes in the world and becomes visible to common man.
-   The term *'Angel of the Lord'*, *'The Lord'*, and *'God'* are interchangeable. *(Exodus 3:1-4)*
-   The *'Angel of the Lord'* is the Holy personage of God appearing in some respects like a human.
-   The *'Angel of the Lord'*, is the visible pre-incarnate manifestation to man in the Old Testament.

THE ADVERSARY

Initially this seems like a strange title, but if we decide to look at the language, we discover quickly that the Hebrew title 'SATAN', actually means 'the adversary'. If one were to write a book about God, some people will be interested. If there is a book on angels, many people will be fascinated. However, typically as humans we seem to be drawn to the love of scary news and if you release any detail on 'Satan', it comes as no surprise that most people will potentially be all over it. It is a shame that the bad guys do get a lot of the press, but an important thing to consider in any kind of warfare, being it spiritual or in the natural, one must know one's enemy (General Sun Tzu). The apostle Paul writes in 2nd Corinthians 2:11, to avoid being ignorant of the devices of Satan:

11 'Lest Satan should get an advantage of us: for we are not ignorant of his devices'.

The first time we see this character emerge is in the Garden of Eden in the first chapters of Genesis. So far we have covered a lot of information on spiritual beings in scripture, so it is only natural to investigate the bad ones. There is no build up in context to where Satan came from: this is why in Jewish tradition the serpent is recognized only as a creature and not as Satan, because the complete back story was not available. A matter of fact, Judaism has no recognition of Satan as an influential figure. They attribute good and bad as coming from humans themselves starting with Adam and Eve. Even in the book of Job, Orthodox Jews view Satan as an angel who accuses a person before God at judgement day as a formality, but the general consensus is that God has it covered (There is no official set doctrine on life after death in Judaism either). Clearly, however, with all scripture and looking at the whole journey of Biblical accounts in both covenants, we can pinpoint Satan as the shape shifting figure in the garden. This back story develops as we gain a fuller and more detailed journey in our learning.

In Genesis 1 God creates a perfect, ordered reality out of chaos and disorder, which is teaming and flourishing with life. Humans are placed in the garden to rule and have dominion over it. They act as his stewards and representatives on earth. His creation is called 'good', 7 times in correlation with the number of days. When God created man, they were called 'very good'. Genesis 3 can be viewed and interpreted as not just a rebellion story by humans, but also by the serpent, as this is where 'the Satan' is introduced to the scene. The serpent was known to be crafty, smart, shrewd and perceptive, possibly indicating a being with a lot of wisdom. This creature is, therefore, clearly set apart as different from the rest of the creatures in the garden and points towards experience and capability. Seemingly blessed more than other creatures, but following the 'fall', cursed among all the creatures of the field in an inversion of what once was, to crawl on its belly for the rest of its days in the dust (Gen 3:14). In Genesis 3 we see God delivering various judgments against those who brought sin into His perfect world. Adam, Eve, and the serpent are all told about the consequences of their rebellion. To the serpent God says:

"And I will put enmity between thee and the woman, and between thy seed and her seed; it shall bruise thy head, and thou shalt bruise his heel" *(Gen 3:15)*

The adversary stood in a state of rebellion towards the Creator (Gangel 2003). At this point in this epic we are not yet informed on why he rebelled. He was reportedly intent on ruining every part of God's project and everything that was good. He forms the first portrait of evil in scripture. God created the good out of chaos and created structure. This mysterious figure comes along and attempts to tumble it back into chaos and darkness. Humanity joins the rebellion which brings about chaos and ultimately death. This is where we have this sense of intertwined rebellion in humanity and the spiritual realm. It is a never-ending pattern that we see emerge repeatedly throughout the Biblical text.

Tradition has attributed this serpent figure to be a creature in disguise, perhaps one of the Cherubim. As I pointed out previously, Seraphim means 'snake', and Isaiah 6 lists these Cherubim as Seraphim. This may indeed be an indication in this wider analysis of scripture that this Cherub is a former member of God's throne room. Ezekiel also understood this individual to be a spiritual entity who went rogue and refused to serve under God's wisdom and authority. This entity wanted to be God or at least His equal, which is the same temptation he puts forward to Adam and Eve. He convinced them that they could have dominion over the world, but on their own terms. This also resulted in them being kicked out of the garden just like Lucifer being cast from heaven. From that moment on he slithered away and started working behind the scenes, orchestrating division between humanity. The adversary has many descriptions from 'serpent', to 'leviathan', or even the 'king of death'. Titles like, 'tempter', 'evil one', 'father of lies', 'prince of the power of the air', or the Greek word Devil 'slanderer', gives us an indication of his function and the way he operates. He accuses man before God at Judgement (Zechariah 3). Beelzebub meaning 'Lord of the Flies', conjures up the image of a defiler of everything that is good and is happy to live and perch on everything that is polluted to spread disease in the mind and body. One of the best interpretations of his function with the prefix 'the', is 'Satan', which pointed out earlier means 'the adversary'. 'The Satan' is not a name, it is a role of antithesis. He is in fact anti everything and seeks to undo structure back into chaos and darkness (Mackie 2021).

The language in scripture upon closer analysis indicates a good figure, going rogue. Amongst all of creation, it would not be unusual to have all God's creatures present during creation, even the Cherubim who later on block the entrance to the Garden of Eden after the fall takes place. This place was sacred space and since God walked and talked with Adam, it may also have been a place in view of the heavenly throne. The account in Genesis portrays 'The Satan', as a fallen figure, just in the same way Adam and Eve are going to be. Every time we have the Hebrew word 'seraph', in the Bible it has a literal meaning of snake. There are 8 examples of this in scripture. It has been theorized that the word can also mean 'burning ones' (Heiser 2018), but we do not have an example of any type of creature on fire, neither a rich history of Bible commentary making it so. Isaiah, however, records flying snakes for 'seraph' 3 times in his writings as 'throne guardians'. This imagery of course has much in common with the cobra as the protector of the Egyptian throne, nonetheless with exaggerated flaps as wings by ancient artists. The idea of 'burning ones', was likely to be attributed to a poisonous snake that bites, or spits its venom. Any such injury would result in agonizing burning emanating from the entrance point of the bite mark, or the eyes due to a cobra spit. The reference of burning is thus likely to be the feeling one experiences from venom. 'Seraph' can mean 'snake', but as a verb it means 'burning'. The comparison with Cherubim is evident, as they can look like bulls, eagles, lions and upon closer analysis of the Hebrew, like 'snakes'.

The interesting thing in Isaiah 14 is when he talks about the ruler of Babylon, who was a king also trying to make his throne ascend above God's realm. Isaiah writes this concerning the adversary:

*"**How you are fallen from heaven,**
O Day Star, son of Dawn!*
How you are cut down to the ground,
you who laid the nations low!
[13] ***You said in your heart,***
*'**I will ascend to heaven;***
above the stars of God
I will set my throne on high;*
I will sit on the mount of assembly*
in the far reaches of the north,[j]
[14] ***I will ascend above the heights of the clouds;***
I will make myself like the Most High.'*
[15] *But you are brought down to Sheol,*
to the far reaches of the pit.
[16] *Those who see you will stare at you*
and ponder over you:
'Is this the man who made the earth tremble,
who shook kingdoms,
[17] *who made the world like a desert*
and overthrew its cities,
who did not let his prisoners go home?'
[18] *All the kings of the nations lie in glory,*
each in his own tomb;[d]
[19] *but you are cast out, away from your grave,*
like a loathed branch,
clothed with the slain, those pierced by the sword,
who go down to the stones of the pit,
like a dead body trampled underfoot. *Isaiah 14:12-19*

Therefore Isaiah 14 is linking directly into the Genesis 3

account as a form or parody or parallel with the adversary. This communicated that the serpent was a heavenly being that disguised itself and deceived the humans. An example of an attempted coup and tempting the humans to follow the same path. Isaiah therefore is very intentional the way he brings the seraphim into the account (14 vs 19) 'trampled underfoot', modelled after the Genesis 3 fall (Mackie 2021).

As you may have discovered, 'The Satan', never receives an actual name. He is, however, endowed with descriptions communicating his function, and a venomous snake is one of them. In Ezekiel 28 he is called a Cherub and reference to a Seraph in Isaiah 14:19. The interesting thing is that the name 'Lucifer' appears nowhere in both original testaments in Hebrew or Greek. This naturally brings us back to Isaiah 14. As Isaiah describes the ruler of Babylon, the description is intended to kill two birds with one stone, as the references are meant to refer to both the human and spiritual ruler. Standing behind the icon or idols of Babylon stands the rebellious spiritual dominion. The ruler of Babylon is thus under a spiritual authority. Isaiah speaks of the ruler of Babylon as the 'morning star' or *'Day Star, son of Dawn'*, depending on which version you read (vs 12). It is in the Cananite mythological phrase 'Helo Ben-Shekhar', meaning the 'shining one' or 'son of the dawn'. We can see the direct correlating with Jupiter and Venus here, making clear descriptions of astronomy. The last star to be seen as the sun comes up is Venus, still in view although the sun is beginning to rise, almost as a testimony of fortitude lingering as long as possible until it is out of view. These planets have invoked many a mythical story of the past. This is what Isaiah is doing as he subtly references these Canaanite epics and does so by linking it to the Genesis 3 account, of the chief rebel whose main desire is to ascend above God's throne and take the place of God himself, rebelling against Yahweh's rule and authority.

As we go forward in time we enter the Roman era and

everything recorded in the Biblia Vulgate is done so in Latin. It is St. Jerome who takes this famous phrase 'Helo Ben-Shekhar', and translates it as 'Luciferas', literally meaning : 'Venus the morning Star'. Therefore, church tradition always associated Isaiah 14 with Lucifer in the Vulgate. This is of course the text where we associate Lucifer falling from heaven like a falling star. The stars were always viewed by those in history as heavenly beings in the sky. Lucifer was never intended to be a name, but it stuck quite well (Mackie, 2021).

In Ezekiel 28:11-19 we have a clear description of something that goes beyond a lament of the King of Tyre, also in the form of a parody. We have no evidence of the King of Tyre having been in Eden, or that he was an 'anointed cherub who covers', neither residing on the 'holy mountain of God', which speaks of sacred space. This parody is therefore a dual prophecy, thus comparing the pride of the King of Tyre to the pride of the adversary. It could also be theorized that the King himself was possessed by the evil one, making a link between the physical and spiritual realm. Rather than recognizing the sovereignty of God, this king attributed his riches to his own wisdom and power. He was not satisfied with what he had been given and wanted more, resulting in Tyre taking advantage of the surrounding nations and expanding its own wealth at the expense of others. In the same way Satan's pride led to his fall and will eventually lead to his final destruction. The prophecy against the city of Tyre was fulfilled in part by the invasion of Nebuchadnezzar (Ezekiel 29:17-21) and brought to its final destruction by the Greeks (Alexander the Great). (Lutzer, 2015)

[11] Moreover, the word of the LORD came to me: [12] "Son of man, raise a lamentation over the king of Tyre, and say to him, Thus says the Lord GOD:

"You were the signet of perfection,[a]
full of wisdom and perfect in beauty.

¹³ *You were in Eden, the garden of God;*
every precious stone was your covering,
sardius, topaz, and diamond,
  beryl, onyx, and jasper,
sapphire,[j] emerald, and carbuncle;
  and crafted in gold were your settings
  and your engravings.[k]
On the day that you were created
  they were prepared.
¹⁴ **You were an anointed guardian cherub.**
  I placed you; you were on the holy mountain of God;
  in the midst of the stones of fire you walked.
¹⁵ *You were blameless in your ways*
  from the day you were created,
  till unrighteousness was found in you.
¹⁶ *In the abundance of your trade*
  you were filled with violence in your midst, and you sinned;
so I cast you as a profane thing from the mountain of
God,
  and I destroyed you,[l] O guardian cherub,
  from the midst of the stones of fire.
¹⁷ *Your heart was proud because of your beauty;*
  you corrupted your wisdom for the sake of your splendor.
I cast you to the ground;
  I exposed you before kings,
  to feast their eyes on you.
¹⁸ *By the multitude of your iniquities,*
  in the unrighteousness of your trade
  you profaned your sanctuaries;
so I brought fire out from your midst;
  it consumed you,
and I turned you to ashes on the earth
  in the sight of all who saw you.
¹⁹ *All who know you among the peoples*
  are appalled at you;
you have come to a dreadful end
  and shall be no more forever." Eziekiel 28:11-19

When unpacking the descriptions of the evil one, 'Satan' seems to be the most popular. It means the adversary or opposer. As mentioned earlier, no actual name should be assigned, as it presupposes the honor and dignity of being named, and Biblical authors do this quite deliberately. This is reminiscent of ignoring an individual to define their worth. We see references of images, titles and descriptions of function, but this biblical character is never formerly named. This encourages us to view this figure as a collage of awful deeds, the antithesis of everything that God calls good with the one desire of plunging everything back into chaos. As with the Cherubim and Seraphim, this figure is stooped in mystery. As mentioned previously, Christian doctrine has largely defined this figure as originally having been a Cherub.

It is the apostle John in the apocalyptic book of Revelation who brings a lot of the imagery we associate with the adversary together into one unified text. In Revelation chapter 12 he says:

'And there was war in heaven: Michael and his angels going forth to war with the dragon; and the dragon warred and his angels; [8] *and they prevailed not, neither was their place found any more in heaven.* [9] *And the **great dragon** was cast down, the **old serpent**, he **that is called the Devil** and **Satan**, the deceiver of the whole* [b] *world; he was cast down to the earth, and his angels were cast down with him'.* [10] *Revelation 12:7-10*

This description in Revelation goes onto reference a 'great dragon' an 'old serpent', the 'devil' and 'Satan' all of which we have already seen in different verses. The apostle John brings a lot of clarity as to this elusive character being talked about from Genesis onwards. John knits all these key descriptions and nouns together to avoid any type of confusion as to who is being referred to, serving as a great summary in the last book of the Bible of this character.

Learning Points

- *The Satan is Hebrew for 'the adversary'.*
- *The adversary forms the first portrait of evil in scripture.*
- *Tradition views the adversary as a fallen Cherub or Seraph.*
- *The description of the adversary often denote function such as 'tempter', 'evil one', Devil 'slanderer', Beelzebub 'Lord of the flies', or untrustworthy creatures such as snakes, leviathan or indeed the king of death.*
- *The adversary seeks to throw everything back into chaos and desctruction, literally a pre-creation state.*
- *'The Satan', never receives an actul name. The Bible largely avoids the adversary with having an actual name, as this presupposes the honour and dignity of being named.*
- *In Ezekiel the adversary is called a Cherub and Seraph in Isaiah.*
- *Church tradition associates Isaiah 14 with Lucifer 'light bearer', in the Vulgate.*
- *The apostle John is the person who ties many descriptions of the adversary together in one verse, knitting everything together in this unfolding story bringing clarity to this elusive spiritual being. 'Great Dragon', 'Old Serpent', called the 'Devil' and 'Satan' (Revelation 12:9).*

DEMONS

Demons come into play when we take another look at the 'Divine Council'. In the Torah we discover that many of these staff members rebelled as well, and the term 'Sons of God', is attributed to these rebellious entities. We have this rather uncomfortable account in Genesis 6, when members of the Divine council 'Sons of God', had been given a role to perform on earth to oversee certain areas. They saw that the daughters of men were fair and decided to leave their abode and mate with women, causing offspring that were known to be Giants and men of renown (Heiser 2020).

6 When man began to multiply on the face of the land and daughters were born to them, ² the sons of God saw that the daughters of man were attractive. And they took as their wives any they chose. ³ Then the LORD said, "My Spirit shall not abide in[a] man forever, for he is flesh: his days shall be 120 years." ⁴ The Nephilim[b] were on the earth in those days, and also afterward, when the sons of God came in to the daughters of man and they bore children to them. These were the mighty men who were of old, the men of renown'. **Genesis 6 1-4 ESV**

They were known as the Nephilim. (Sidenote: A lot of Greek mythology is full of these demi God accounts eg: the Titans that were imprisoned in darkness, including other historical epics revered in Hinduism speaking of Giants and Demon Kings) There are naturally many characters in the Bible that bring about a certain level of awe and fascination, but by far these come across as the most strange and disturbing. Strange to us, but the ancients who wrote this information down and recorded it in history, plus the people who read it, did not have a problem as viewing it as accurate history. These scary beings make an appearance in a lot of accounts in the Biblical narratives. Even historians after the second temple period record such beings: This would seem highly unlikely if we were to view the spirit world and the physical world as unrelated separate realms, but there exists this overlap and the Bible accounts do teach us that spiritual beings do enter the physical realm, even if to sit down and eat (Abraham and the three visitors Gen: 18).

18 And the LORD appeared to him by the oaks[a] of Mamre, as he sat at the door of his tent in the heat of the day. ² He lifted up his eyes and looked, and behold, three men were standing in front of him. When he saw them, he ran from the tent door to meet them and bowed himself to the earth ³ and said, "O Lord,[b] if I have found favor in your sight, do not pass by your servant. ⁴ Let a little water be brought, and wash your feet, and rest yourselves under the tree, ⁵ while I bring a morsel of bread, that you may refresh yourselves, and after that you may pass on—since you have come to your servant." So they said, "Do as you have said." **Genesis 18: 1-4**

In the account of Sodom and Gomorrah we see this overlap between the physical and spiritual again in Genesis 19, as the inhabitants take a shine sexually to the two Hosts of Heaven who came to save Lot and his family before destroying the city. They viewed these angels as normal human beings.

19 The two angels came to Sodom in the evening, and Lot was sitting in the gate of Sodom. When Lot saw them, he rose to meet them and bowed himself with his face to the earth ² and said, "My lords, please turn aside to your servant's house and spend the night and wash your feet. Then you may rise up early and go on your way." They said, "No; we will spend the night in the town square." ³ But he pressed them strongly; so they turned aside to him and entered his house. And he made them a feast and baked unleavened bread, and they ate.

⁴ But before they lay down, the men of the city, the men of Sodom, both young and old, all the people to the last man, surrounded the house. ⁵ And they called to Lot, "Where are the men who came to you tonight? Bring them out to us, that we may know them." ⁶ Lot went out to the men at the entrance, shut the door after him, ⁷ and said, "I beg you, my brothers, do not act so wickedly. **Genesis 19: 1-7**

This overlap between spiritual beings and physical requirements potentially being fulfilled, blurs the lines of normal understanding. In the Old Testament, whenever you have the reference of 'Sons of God', you know scripture is talking about spiritual beings, including 'Hosts of Heaven'. The events of Genesis 6 are confirmed by Jude who wrote the epistle of Jude. He links these accounts of the 'Sons of God', with Sodom and Gomorrah. Jude speaks of disobedient angels that did not keep their abode, not keeping their proper domain. He informs us that these entities are kept in eternal bonds in a place of darkness awaiting judgement. (Jude even mentions the name 'Enoch', in Jude 1:14) He is linking Genesis 6 with 19.

⁵ Now I want to remind you, although you once fully knew it, that Jesus, who saved[a] a people out of the land of Egypt, afterward destroyed those who did not believe. ⁶ And the angels who did not stay within their own position of authority, but left their proper dwelling, he has kept in eternal chains under gloomy darkness until the judgment of the great day— ⁷ just as Sodom and Gomorrah and the surrounding cities, which likewise indulged in sexual immorality and pursued unnatural desire,[b] serve as an example by undergoing a punishment of eternal fire. **Jude 5-7**

This is clearly how Jude understood these accounts and so did all the others in the faith during his day, inclusive of the writings found in the Dead Sea Scrolls. The Apostle Peter is also without question making reference to these same accounts and linking them. No doubt Peter was fully aware what was written in some of the second temple literature.

⁴For if God did not spare angels when they sinned, but cast them into hell[a] and committed them to chains[b] of gloomy darkness to be kept until the judgment; ⁵if he did not spare the ancient world, but preserved Noah, a herald of righteousness, with seven others, when he brought a flood upon the world of the ungodly; ⁶if by turning the cities of Sodom and Gomorrah to ashes he condemned them to extinction, making them an example of what is going to happen to the ungodly;[c] ⁷and if he rescued righteous Lot, greatly distressed by the sensual conduct of the wicked ⁸(for as that righteous man lived among them day after day, he was tormenting his righteous soul over their lawless deeds that he saw and heard); ⁹then the Lord knows how to rescue the godly from trials,[d] and to keep the unrighteous under punishment until the day of judgment, ¹⁰and especially those who indulge[k] in the lust of defiling passion and despise authority. **2 Peter 2:4-10**

This is also the Jewish world view during the second temple period and after, as the historical writer Josephus writes:

*"For many angels (11- This notion, that the fallen angels were, in some sense, the fathers of the old giants, was the constant opinion of antiquity.) of God accompanied with women, and begat sons that proved unjust, and despisers of all that was good, on account of the confidence they had in their own strength; for the tradition is, that these men did what resembled the acts of those whom the **Grecians call giants**." (Josephus, Antiquities of the Jews, Chapter 3)*

Josephus is not just considered an average historian: he was the authority and reliability most of Roman history of his period relies upon. Josephus' works have also been used to verify Biblical accounts should historians reject the historicity of

Jesus.

The book of Enoch which counts as second temple literature was well understood by Jews during the intertestamental period and records the accounts from Genesis 6 in similar, albeit more detail in Enoch Chapter 7. I have included further Biblical parallel references to convey similarities in the accepted canon:

1 And they took wives for themselves and everyone chose for himself one each. And they began to go into them and were promiscuous with them. And they taught them charms and spells, and they showed them the cutting of roots and trees.

2 And they became pregnant and bore large giants. And their height was three thousand cubits.
(Genesis 6:1-4), (Numbers 13:30-33), (Deuteronomy 2:10-12), (Deuteronomy 2:19-21),
(Deuteronomy 3:11), (2 Samuel 21:16), (2 Samuel 21:18-22),

3 These devoured all the toil of men; until men were unable to sustain them.

4 And the giants turned against them in order to devour men.

5 And they began to sin against birds, and against animals, and against reptiles, and against fish, and they devoured one another's flesh, and drank the blood from it.

6 Then the Earth complained about the lawless ones.
(Genesis 6:5-13)

If we view other writings of the ancients from pre- Babylonian times including the epics of Gilgamesh, we see this titan being exhibited as a giant, towering over a lion in one arm and in many other statues holding a snake in the other. Gilgamesh was the founder of the city of Uruk. He is also referenced in the book of Giants, which was one of the fragment scrolls found in the Dead Sea Scrolls showing striking similarities to the book of Enoch.

(Statue of Gilgamesh in San Francisco)

So there exists this whole tradition of giant demi-gods who are mighty men and kings of epic proportions. King David and his strong men wiped out the last remnant of them (2 Samuel 21:15-22). Every child who has been to Sunday school knows of the account of David slaying Goliath (1 Samuel 17). If we consider the Dead Sea Scrolls, including the book of 'Enoch', 'Giants', 'Jubilees', 'The wisdom of Ben Sira', and Jude, we cannot escape the disturbing fact that Genesis 6 was not just an inference of a deed, it was factually laying down for us as something that happened between 'The Sons of God', and human women resulting in this terrible offspring. Other interpretations of scripture only developed through later traditions of the Church, as biblical accounts were no longer viewed through the lens of Judaism. Catholicism, the Great Schism and the Reformation, were completely at odds with the actual world view in its original context. Later theologies including R. C. Sproul excused Genesis 6 as a commentary based on the Godly lineage of Seth mixing with the ungodly lineage of Cain (Sproul 2011). Scripture, however, does not encourage this as genealogies are recorded with great detail to avoid misconceptions, so this theory is simply used to explain away something which comes across as very uncomfortable.

St Augustine and St Jerome did not adhere to the original Jewish worldview. However, Ireneaus did seem to grasp the original interpretation. Irenaeus was the bishop of the church in what is now Lyons, France. He was a disciple of Polycarp, who was a disciple of the Apostle John. His treatise *Against Heresies* was a vital piece of work that challenged the heretical Gnostic Christianity that threatened the true faith at that time. Regarding the Genesis 6 dilemma he wrote:

"And for a very long while wickedness extended and spread, and reached and laid hold upon the whole race of mankind, until a very small seed of righteousness remained among them and illicit unions took place upon the earth, since angels were united with the daughters of the race of mankind; and they bore to them sons who for their exceeding greatness were called **giants.***" (*A Discourse in the Demonstration of Apostolic Preaching; 18)

Another first century church father was Clement of Rome. He was a Christian bishop in Rome and was a contemporary of the Apostle John. His epistle to the Corinthian church is one of the oldest existing Christian writings outside of the New Testament. The Clementine Homilies are a series of writings from the 2nd and 3rd century claiming to record dialogue between Clement and the Apostle Peter. Although the authorship is questioned, its details on the Nephilim again demonstrate that this concept and understanding was well established in the thinking of the early church. Clement also seems to describe how they assumed bodily forms, thereby leaving their former dwelling place.

"But when, having assumed these forms, they convicted as covetous those who stole them, and changed themselves into the nature of men, in order that, living holily, and showing the possibility of so living, they might subject the ungrateful to punishment, yet having become in all respects men, they also partook of human lust, and being brought under its subjection they fell into cohabitation with women; and being involved with them, and sunk in defilement and altogether emptied of their first power, were unable to turn back to the first purity of their proper nature, their members turned away from their fiery substance: for the fire itself, being extinguished by the weight of lust, and changed *into flesh, they trode the impious path downward. For they themselves, being fettered with the bonds of flesh, were constrained and strongly bound; wherefore they have no more been able to ascend into the heavens."* (*Clementine Homilies, Homily VIII,* Chapter XIII).

Surrounding Israel were ancient Kingdoms that were protected by these enormous warrior kings who in themselves were part human, part 'Sons of God', and possessed divine wisdom beyond that of normal mortal man. The authors of scripture, however, do not encourage these beings to be honored, as they were part human rebels captured in darkness. These kings spread unimaginable violence and one of those kings goes on to build the city which we will forever associate with an evil kingdom and that is Babylon in Genesis 10. The builder of this great city was Nimrod and his name is associated with the word 'rebel'. This kingdom is the third large scale rebellion or fall where they build a big tower attempting to make a name for themselves, but God scatters them. Many historians have theorized that Nimrod and Gilgamesh may have been the same historical figure.

It is Moses who brings a lot more context to this situation when he lets us know that it was this particular rebellion that prompted God to hand over the nations to the rebellious hosts of heaven, the gods of money, sex, power and violence (Deuteronomy 32:8).

When the Most High gave to the nations their inheritance, when he divided mankind, he fixed the borders[a] of the peoples according to the number of the **sons of God**. *Deuteronomy 32:8*

Moses is the first person to assign the word 'demons', to these 'Heavenly Hosts', as they were considered as lesser spiritual beings (Prof. Ben. Dov 2014). So, if we view the world and its corruption, we need to know and understand that it is actually these demonic entities that are behind the chaos. They are not just responsible for this widespread chaos in societies, but also on a personal level where they exploit and entice human flesh in greed and selfishness, not just humanity's carnal nature, but also infirmities. Anything that works as the antithesis of God's good creation is attributed to demons and 'The Satan', as they attempt to force creation back into chaos, disorder, darkness and death. This is the main reason Jesus makes it clear that his enemy is not humanity, he came to save us from the power of the adversary. Jesus knew that it would cost him everything at every level to defeat death itself and that is what he did.

Demons in Jewish culture could not be cast out; this is why they were so surprised when Jesus was able to do so. There exists no Old Testament example of anyone casting out a demon. However, David was able through anointed music to settle the spirit of King Saul when he was plagued by them:

[14] Now the Spirit of the LORD departed from Saul, and a harmful spirit from the LORD tormented him. [15] And Saul's servants said to him, "Behold now, a harmful spirit from God is tormenting you. [16] Let our lord now command your servants who are before you to seek out a man who is skillful in playing the lyre, and when the harmful spirit from God is upon you, he will play it, and you will be well." [17] **1 Samuel 16:14-16**

The evidence we have covered shows us clearly the origin of high level spiritual entities. However, we are still left with an important question: **Where do demon spirits come from?**

It was well understood by the ancients, that the origin of demons, was not specifically the 'watchers' that were assigned geographical locations, neither the entities that fell from heaven. Second temple Judaism understood that demons were disembodied spirits of the Nephilim, the wicked offspring of the 'Sons of God'. To put it simply, these giants were never a part of God's original creation, as they were a product of spiritual beings and humans resulting in human hybrids. When these beings turned on one another and died, their evil spirits had nowhere to go. They did not qualify for Sheol (the realm of the dead) and they were not chained up with the disobedient angels that left their first abode. They were therefore roaming the earth seeking to be re-embodied again, searching for an entry point, whether human or animal. Their nature is as evil as their actions when their bodies were alive on earth (Heiser 2020).

This does stray quite far from traditional Christian orthodoxy, but this theory was first put forward to me as a possibility during a lecture decades ago at bible college. For serious Bible students, Dr Heiser's arguments are based on ancient semitic and eastern materials. His central argument is the explanation of three divine rebellions against God. Traditional orthodoxy only looks at the Fall in the Garden of Eden, which is mainly Augustinian. Dr Heiser characterizes the first fall as (1) Satan's initial rebellion against God, secondly (2) 'The Sons of God', in Genesis 6 leaving their remit and taking human wives. Finally the third rebellion (3) as the 'Divine Council', being given territorial rule over the nations, but deciding to take the glory for themselves and going rogue. This three fold framework does explain most of the Bible's spiritual warfare passages and it thus makes that clear distinction between 'the Satan', 'false gods' and 'demons'. I will delve more deeply into this Enochian worldview in the chapter explaining the book of Enoch, and how it puts Genesis 6 into context.

Learning Points

- *'Sons of God', are always titles for fallen 'Divine Council members'.*
- *Second Temple Judaism believed in the Genesis 6 account, whereby spiritual beings had offspring with human women.*
- *Second Temple Judaism understood that demons were disembodied spirits of the Nephilim, the wicked offspring of the 'Sons of God'.*
- *This is not just documented in Second Temple writings, but also Josephus who was a Jewish historian employed by Rome.*
- *After their desctruction, the spirits of these angelic/human hybrids had nowhere to go. They did not qualify for Sheol as they were never meant to be created and did not follow their fathers who were locked in chains until judgement. These spirits therefore roam the earth seeking to be re-embodied again, searching for any entry point, whether beast or man.*
- *Early church fathers such as Irenaeus and Clemente supported the Enochian world view.*
- *Second temple Judaism does not just recognise one Fall, but three divine falls. The first fall as (1) Satan's initial rebellion against God, secondly (2) 'The Sons of God', in Genesis 6 leaving their remit and taking human wives. Finally the third rebellion (3) as*

the 'divine council', being given territorial rule over the nations, but deciding to take the glory for themselves and going rogue.

ANGELS NAMED IN SCRIPTURE

Names are naturally very important and we derive meaning from names, which makes the naming of a child especially important, as it carries with itself identity. These meanings naturally are very relevant in scripture and open up enormous detail in regard to patriarchs and spiritual beings. It is interesting at this point, that the only two specific names mentioned in scripture in regard to angels in the canon of 66 books are: 'Gabriel' and 'Michael'. There is no other record of a specific name of an angel serving God in the protestant canon. We have covered 'The Angel of the Lord', already in a previous chapter and concluded that this person is Jesus, before the incarnation. Gabriel means 'God is my power', and Michael means 'Who is like God?'. The important learning point as to prevent any kind of worship of these heavenly hosts is the meaning of their names themselves. Both Gabriel's name and the name of Michael do not point to the majesty of the spiritual being, but to the glory of God himself. As humans who are created in the image and likeness of God, angels are thus images of both his presence and his power (Mackie 2019). This is how the 'Sons of God', fell as reported in Deuteronomy, because these overseers sought glory for themselves, thereby sentencing their lives to everlasting separation from God. Yahweh does not provide a process of redemption for rebellious members of his 'Heavenly Host'.

The whole topic of angels is of course very fascinating, but also comes with a strong warning. We are not encouraged to look for them. If they have a mission or are given a message for the people of God, they find us! Needless to say the supportive role they play is to re-establish the Kingdom of God on earth and to help fulfill God's plan. Angels are therefore used to show the way and serve the people of God. Most of the time, one isn't even going to know about their presence, neither their supernatural intervention in the natural realm. This is the very reason why only two of the 'Angelic Host' faithful to God are mentioned specifically by name in scripture.

Michael is specifically described as an archangel in scripture. We see him referenced in the books of Daniel 10:13; 21, Jude 1:9 and Revelation 12:7. Michael is always associated as a high ranking powerful angel who engages in spiritual battles. He is an archangel, deriving from the Greek word 'archangelos', meaning 'chief' or 'ruler'. The Bible suggests there is a ranking system of the angelic host and it is clear that Michael would stand at the top of that. Daniel 10:13 describes Michael as one of the 'Chief Princes', which may indicate that there are other archangels too, but this is inferred instead of being clearly evidential. It is safe to assume that amongst this leadership structure he stands at the top of the Angelic Host.

[13] 'The prince of the kingdom of Persia withstood me twenty-one days, but Michael, **one of the chief princes**, *came to help me, for I was left there with the kings of Persia'.* **Daniel 10:13 ESV**

If we look at Jude 1:9, the definite article is used which promotes the singular form, prompting us to believe that he may indeed be the only archangel.

[9] But when **the** *archangel Michael, contending with the devil, was*

disputing about the body of Moses, he did not presume to pronounce a blasphemous judgment, but said, "The Lord rebuke you." Jude 1:9 ESV

In Daniel 10:21, Michael is described as 'your prince', by another angel. This specific angel is talking to Daniel who is Jewish: therefore, Michael is seen as the force overseeing the protection of the Jewish people. This is confirmed by Daniel 12:1:

12 "At that time shall arise Michael, **the great prince** *who has charge of your people. And there shall be a time of trouble, such as never has been since there was a nation till that time. But at that time your people shall be delivered, everyone whose name shall be found written in the book'.* **Daniel 12:1 ESV**

Perhaps there are other archangels protecting other nations, but we are not told about this in scripture: neither are their names mentioned. It is clear that the fallen angels mentioned in earlier chapters in this book have been assigned territories, taking from the Deuteronomy 32 world view. One of these is named as the 'Prince of Greece', including a 'Prince of Persia'. It was the 'Prince of Persia', preventing the angel delivering the message to Daniel, whereby the archangel Michael intervened.

20 Then he said, "Do you know why I have come to you? But now I will return to fight against the prince of Persia; and when I go out, behold, the prince of Greece will come'. **Daniel 10:20 ESV**

It is clear to see throughout Daniel chapter 10 that the archangel's duty is to engage in spiritual combat. We see in 1 Thessalonians 4:16-18, that the archangel is involved in the eschatological proceedings of Christ coming back for his church:

16 'For the Lord himself will descend from heaven with a cry of command, with the **voice of an archangel**, *and with the sound of the trumpet of God. And the dead in Christ will rise first. 17 Then we who are alive, who* *are left, will be caught up together with them in the clouds to meet the Lord in the air, and so we will always be with the Lord.* [18] *Therefore encourage one another with these words'.* **1 Thessalonians 4:16-18 ESV**

In Jude 1:9 we have the very brief account of the archangel Michael contending with the adversary over the body of Moses. We have a distinct impression that Michael is holding off this engagement until the appointed time. It is clear that Michael is operating in the field of his sphere of influence and is cautious not overstep the mark, although one may get the impression that he is giving the adversary a heads up: ie 'You just wait, your time will come'!

[9] *But when the archangel Michael, contending with the devil, was disputing about the body of Moses, he did not presume to pronounce a blasphemous judgment, but said, "The Lord rebuke you." Jude 1:9 ESV*

In Jewish tradition there exists more information in pseudepigraphic literature recorded in 'The Testament of Abraham', whereby Michael is described as escorting believers to the afterlife, which is also characteristic of the dispute Michael had with the adversary regarding the body of Moses.

'And immediately **Michael** *the archangel stood beside him with multitude of angels, and they bore his precious soul in their hands in divinely woven linen. And they tended the body of the righteous Abraham with divine ointments and perfumes until the third day after his death. And they buried him in the promised land at the oak of Mamre, while the angels escorted his precious soul and ascended into heaven singing the thrice-holy hymn to God, the master of all, and they see it (down) for the worship of the God and Father'.* (Testament of Abraham 20:10-12, Recension A)

The last references we have of the archangel Michael are in the book of Revelation 12:7. It is traditionally depicted in eschatology as an epic war being fought at the end of time: however, the timeline is not that clear. We have Michael and his angels fighting against 'The Dragon', and this Dragon and his angels are fighting back. The Dragon is defeated and thrown to the earth. The adversary uses all his strength to wage war against the Saints and anyone holding fast to the testimony of Jesus:

*⁷ Now war arose in heaven, **Michael** and his angels fighting against the dragon. And the dragon and his angels fought back, ⁸ but he was defeated, and there was no longer any place for them in heaven. ⁹ And the great dragon was thrown down, that ancient serpent, who is called the devil and Satan, the deceiver of the whole world—he was thrown down to the earth, and his angels were thrown down with him. ¹⁰ And I heard a loud voice in heaven, saying, "Now the salvation and the power and the kingdom of our God and the authority of his Christ have come, for the accuser of our brothers[a] has been thrown down, who accuses them day and night before our God. ¹¹ And they have conquered him by the blood of the Lamb and by the word of their testimony, for they loved not their lives even unto death. ¹² Therefore, rejoice, O heavens and you who dwell in them! But woe to you, O earth and sea, for the devil has come down to you in great wrath, because he knows that his time is short!"*

*¹³ And when the dragon saw that he had been thrown down to the earth, he pursued the woman who had given birth to the male child. ¹⁴ But the woman was given the two wings of the great eagle so that she might fly from the serpent into the wilderness, to the place where she is to be nourished for a time, and times, and half a time. ¹⁵ The serpent poured water like a river out of his mouth after the woman, to sweep her away with a flood. ¹⁶ But the earth came to the help of the woman, and the earth opened its mouth and swallowed the river that the dragon had poured from his mouth. ¹⁷ Then the dragon became furious with the woman and went off to make war on the rest of her offspring, on those who keep the commandments of God and hold to the testimony of Jesus. And he stood[b] on the sand of the sea'. **Revelation 12:7-17 ESV**

There are a number of interpretations to this scripture. Some view this as an event depicting the birth of Jesus, or indeed the birth of Israel as a nation and offspring of people of whom

Michael is the protector.

The other named angel in scripture as previously mentioned is Gabriel. He is always associated with bringing an important message from God. We see his first appearance in the book of Daniel (8:16), then in the New Testament he appears to Zechariah in the temple (Luke 1:19) announcing the soon coming birth of John the Baptist and finally the annunciation to the Virgin Mary (Luke 1:31). As far as messages go, he has the top job and clearly delivers the most important ones.

Gabriel's first appearance is to the prophet Daniel, and his role is to explain the vision Daniel is trying to grasp (Daniel 8:16). Gabriel's appearance was in the likeness of a man (Daniel 8:15, 9:21).

15'When I, Daniel, had seen the vision, I sought to understand it. And behold, there stood before me one having the **appearance of a man***'. Daniel 8:15*

21'while I was speaking in prayer, the man Gabriel, whom I had seen in the vision at the first, came to me in swift flight at the time of the evening sacrifice'. **Daniel 9:21**

The wording of swift flight, many interpret as having swooped down with wings, but this is not clear from the text. The 'appearance of a man', or 'the man Gabriel', is likely to rule this out. This appearance of Gabriel was clearly something to behold, as Daniel was not just terrified and fell down before him, but also sick for a number of days after the dramatic encounter (Daniel 8:27).

27And I, Daniel, was overcome and lay sick for some days. Then I rose and went about the king's business, but I was appalled by the vision and did not understand it'. Daniel 8:27)

A few chapters on we see another encounter takes place as

Daniel beholds someone who has the likeness of man, likely to have been Gabriel. As the angel is present to help him understand this next vision the pattern becomes fairly clear.

[16] 'And behold, one in the likeness of the children of man touched my lips. Then I opened my mouth and spoke. I said to him who stood before me, "O my lord, by reason of the vision pains have come upon me, and I retain no strength'. **Daniel 10:16**

In this chapter there are clearly a number of angels present. One of these was Michael who aided the angel in delivering the message, defeating the 'Prince of Persia' and 'Prince of Greece'. This gives us a good glimpse into the spiritual realm as it confirms the wars that go on in the unseen dimensions that overlap with the natural world. Gabriel was dispatched as an immediate reaction to Daniel's prayer (Daniel 10:12), but was delayed by 21 days until receiving help from the archangel Michael.

Gabriel's next appearance we see in the temple to the priest Zechariah, who was the soon to be father of John the Baptist. Zechariah was officiating at the altar and Gabriel appeared at the right hand side of the altar of incense, indicating that his prayers had been acknowledged and received.:

'Now while he was serving as priest before God when his division was on duty, [9] according to the custom of the priesthood, he was chosen by lot to enter the temple of the Lord and burn incense. [10] And the whole multitude of the people were praying outside at the hour of incense. [11] And there appeared to him an angel of the Lord standing on the right side of the altar of incense. [12] And Zechariah was troubled when he saw him, and fear fell upon him. [13] But the angel said to him, "Do not be afraid, Zechariah, for your prayer has been heard, and your wife Elizabeth will bear you a son, and you shall call his name John. [14] And you will have joy and gladness, and many will rejoice at his birth, [15] for he will be great before the Lord. And he must not drink wine or strong drink, and he will be filled with the Holy Spirit, even from his mother's womb. [16] And he will turn many of the children of Israel to the Lord their God, [17] and he will go before him in the spirit and power of Elijah, to turn the

hearts of the fathers to the children, and the disobedient to the wisdom of the just, to make ready for the Lord a people prepared."

*[18] And Zechariah said to the angel, "How shall I know this? For I am an old man, and my wife is advanced in years." [19] And the angel answered him, "I am **Gabriel**. I stand in the presence of God, and I was sent to speak to you and to bring you this good news. [20] And behold, you will be silent and unable to speak until the day that these things take place, because you did not believe my words, which will be fulfilled in their time." [21] And the people were waiting for Zechariah, and they were wondering at his delay in the temple. [22] And when he came out, he was unable to speak to them, and they realized that he had seen a vision in the temple. And he kept making signs to them and remained mute. [23] And when his time of service was ended, he went to his home.*

*[24] After these days his wife Elizabeth conceived, and for five months she kept herself hidden, saying, [25] "Thus the Lord has done for me in the days when he looked on me, to take away my reproach among people'. **Luke 1:8-25***

Zachariah's wife Elizabeth was old and advanced in years and was unable to conceive. This angelic vision and message formed a miracle and clear intervention by God to allow this couple to have a son, furthermore someone who would fulfill the prophecy of the coming Elijah who would prepare a way for the Lord. Zachariah was struck speechless until John was 8 days old, in keeping with the law of circumcision and the naming of the child.

Our next appearance of Gabriel is during the time of Elizabeth's pregnancy. This is the annunciation to the Virgin Mary of the incarnation and birth of the Messiah. This unsuspecting woman was called blessed and highly favored by the Most High and was told that the fruit of her womb was to fulfill the Davidic covenant.

*In the sixth month the angel **Gabriel** was sent from God to a city of Galilee named Nazareth, [27] to a virgin betrothed[b] to a man whose name was Joseph, of the house of David. And the virgin's name was Mary. [28] And he came to her and said, "Greetings, O favored one, the Lord is with you!"[c] [29] But she was greatly troubled at the saying, and tried to discern what sort of greeting this might be. [30] And the angel said to her, "Do not be afraid, Mary, for you have found favor with God. [31] And behold, you will conceive in your womb and bear a son, and you shall call his name Jesus. [32] He will be great and will be called the Son of the Most High. And the Lord God will give to him the throne of his father David, [33] and he will reign over the house of Jacob forever, and of his kingdom there will be no end."*

[34] And Mary said to the angel, "How will this be, since I am a virgin?"[d]

[35] And the angel answered her, "The Holy Spirit will come upon you, and the power of the Most High will overshadow you; therefore the child to be born[e] will be called holy—the Son of God. [36] And behold, your relative Elizabeth in her old age has also conceived a son, and this is the sixth month with her who was called barren. [37] For nothing will be impossible with God." [38] And Mary said, "Behold, I am the servant[f] of the Lord; let it be to me according to your word." And the angel departed from her.
Luke 1:26-38

It is interesting to note, that Mary received the message with faith, being overshadowed by the Holy Spirit and thereby conceiving the Saviour. Zechariah was struck dumb due to a lack of faith and human reasoning, however, then carried out the instructions by faith and Elizabeth conceived. In all three specific accounts that mention Gabriel, we have an awe inspiring being, yet an encounter that brings comfort and joy. Gabriel is clearly a highly ranked and trusted angel, who stands in the presence of God and delivers vitally important messages to those who are willing to be used by Him (Sproul 2011).

Learning Points

- *The only named angels in scripture are Michael and Gabriel in the protestant canon of 66 books*
- *Gabriel means 'God is my Power'.*
- *Michael means 'Who is like God'?*
- *Both names point to the majesty of God, not the spiritual being.*
- *Michael is specifically referred to as an archangel.*
- *Michael is a warrior archangel and a chieftain.*
- *Michael is the force overseeing the Jewish people.*
- *Michael took on the 'Prince of Persia', and 'Prince of Greece', in sprititual combat.*
- *Michael and his angels were responsible for throwing the Great Dragon out of heaven (Rev 12).*
- *Gabriel is always associated with bringing the most important messages to earth, whether to Daniel, Zechariah or Mary.*
- *Gabriel can appear with the likeness of a man, but be quite terrifying in the appearance of light.*

THE BOOK OF ENOCH

The first question people may ask about the book of Enoch is linked to the listed Canon. It is not considered part of the inspired 66 books in the protestant Bible, neither part of the Catholic Bible of 73 books, so why is it still considered important to many Christians? (Sidenote: The Catholic Bible lists 3 angels as archangels which are Michael, Gabriel and Raphael). 1st Enoch predates the Christian era and has a lot to teach us. Academia refers to this literature as Second Temple Judaism which is the era in-between the Old Testament and New Testament, otherwise also known as the intertestamental period. The book of Enoch is also classified as pseudepigrapha.

The book of Enoch is relevant, because the New Testament writers would have been fully aware of the content of the book of Enoch. The Jews would have looked at the Hebrew Bible as the inspired word of God, but also wrote loads of commentary on it, attempting to link accounts in scripture to establish connections and meanings (Lumpkin 2011). This second temple literature including Enoch thus becomes visible in the New Testament as it warranted vast discussions in the early church. This does not mean that Enoch is officially inspired and should be part of the canon, but equally this does not diminish its relevance in view of the prominence shown to it by the Jews of that era. It may be interesting to point out, that it is very well worth reading the same material that Biblical writers read for the purpose of understanding the context of the time. Questions need to be asked as to where the Biblical writer's content comes from, what their goal was in communicating certain issues on specific topics, which in turn makes us more literate readers of scripture. Of course in view of the aim of this book, it does have a lot of relevance to angelology, as far more names of spiritual beings are mentioned, not just Michael and Gabriel in the protestant canon, or the addition of Raphael in the Catholic Bible.

The first book of Enoch does get a lot of attention, as there were those in the early church who did really feel that it should have been part of the canon. It did not become part of the canon, because it can't just be linked to a historical prophetic figure of the Bible, but also the account of the individual must be witnessed in the holy language of Hebrew. When viewing the Dead Sea scrolls, there are no Hebrew examples of the book. There exist some Aramaic fragments of Enoch, furthermore, a sect called the Qumran sect who held these books as sacred. This sect wrote commentaries on Enoch and other Temple scrolls. This lets us know that these books did have an important status in the religious community. Had the book of Enoch been available in Hebrew, it would have received a lot more merit.

This, however, did not concern the early church, as the early church largely consisted of Gentiles and the New Testament was written in Greek. A matter of fact, even if we look at the early Church Fathers, very few of them could actually read Hebrew. They thus were able to look at 1st Enoch and see striking resemblance in content mirroring the information in the New Testament. Those who supported the inclusion of Enoch in scripture eventually died out, and the subject was never really effectively resurrected. The majority rejected the book, but still counted it as an important piece of literature. A matter of fact, as we have already discovered, Irenaeus one of the earliest Church Fathers actually quotes Enoch in his writings (Schaff 1885). After a period of time Enoch lost popularity and effectively fell out of use. There was no longer a need for people to read their New Testament in light of intertestamental literature, neither was there an important emphasis placed upon it.

The focus points for theological discussions became the questions church fathers faced in their own day, rather than criticisms of books that had not made it into the inspired canon. We are more sensitive today attempting to read scripture in its original context, because we have the means to do so. We are naturally drawn to primary sources that were not available to theologians of the medieval age, and the Dead Sea Scrolls would be among them.

When tackling the content of the book of Enoch, it could be described as an apocalyptic book. The book is of course pre-Christian, so naturally Jesus is not a point of reference, but it does have messiah figures in these apocalypses. It addresses eschatology and a very major question, which is why the world is being brought to an end, giving substance to the act of judgement. The rejection of the righteousness of God is a strong theme in this material. Enoch traces that line of thinking partly to the Fall in the Garden, but as you have read earlier on, a large part of the transgressions find their root cause in the sin of the 'Watchers', otherwise known as high level elohim (spiritual beings) misusing authority given to them by God. This is the contextual account of Genesis 6 in an Enochian version of that event. (Michael Heiser, A Companion to the Book of Enoch: A Reader's Commentary, Vol I: The Book of the Watchers (1 Enoch 1-36, 2020)

Enoch gives a rational why the world has become so intensely evil and corrupt, which really helps to explain why God has reached the point to why he regrets that He had created man.

Enoch includes the theme of apocalyptic thinking, an explanation of the proliferation of depravity leading to judgement. Enoch is transported to the heavenly throne room of God where he experiences different levels of heaven, with striking similarities to the revelations of John. This experience is enhanced by angelic guides and interpreters clarifying Enoch's experiences. Any literal pieces of work with a strong emphasis on the angelic is often classified by scholars as Enochian, because these elohim feature more heavily in this book than in any other book in the accepted canon.

The next question we gravitate towards regarding the book of Enoch is naturally authenticity in authorship. No actual text trail can be traced back to Enoch himself. The oldest existing text trail for Enoch is in the 3rd century BC as that is consistent with the Aramaic fragments they are found in. The book receives its name, not because of the person who wrote it, but because of the main character who features in it.

The most interesting evidence we can find on the validity of Enoch, are the New Testament books that seem to be informed by Enoch and include important themes in their writing. Jude, 2nd Peter and Revelation have clear distinctions of Enochian scripting. Connection points with the Gospels can also be explored and found, not necessarily word for word, but rather in theme. John who authored the book of revelation borrows heavily from the Old Testament, but no direct quote word for word. John alludes to things by throwing a number of words in a sentence connecting the dots and bringing a lot of questions together. When John is writing, he takes it for granted that the reader knows their Old Testament inside out so does not need to take up the time to quote directly. It is interesting that the 'Book of Life' does not have any roots in the Old Testament, but rather in second temple literature in the intertestamental period just like Enoch. It comes as no surprise that a lot of John's heavenly imagery can also be found in the book of Enoch. It is the specific content that gives it a way, not word for word quotations. The 'Lake of fire' is in

Revelation 19, Matthew 25, but also features in Enoch (Enoch 67:4). It is also fascinating to see references of 'Son of Man', in Enoch which is Jesus' main description about himself in the Gospels (Enoch 71:14). This description was sufficient for Caiaphas to condemn Jesus to death at the trial in the Sanhedrin. Many historians have criticized scripture on the grounds of a messiah figure only being introduced later on in church teaching, but nevertheless this idea already pre-existed in the second temple literature of Enoch.

When reviewing the topic of the Watchers (fallen angels) it is the book of 1st Enoch 10:11-13 that described their demise and imprisonment. This can also be linked into the book of Revelation 9:1-10 (Heiser 2020), which is theorized by many theologians as a clear parallel. This is an account of the release of these demonic beings upon the earth as a judgement, leading to the end of the world and judgement day itself.

In all Jewish traditions about the events of Genesis 6:1-4 concerning the 'Sons of God', or as Enoch would describe 'the Watchers', or 'Angels', the disembodied spirits of the giants (Nephilim) are viewed as demons in the Gospels and as the spiritual beings Jesus encounters when he casts them out. We find that the offending beings 'the watchers', are sent back to the pit or abyss and imprisoned until the end of days. This eschatological endpoint exists in Jewish tradition itself. In other words, they are in jail. Revelation 9 describes the opening of the abyss and the release of these demonic powers, specifically the ones that were imprisoned. To anyone familiar with intertestamental literature it is frightfully obvious who these beings are that are released upon the earth. The reason why this is such a big deal, is that they speed up the depravity process of human kind and are linked to the authors of idolatry. Many scholars would suggest this, as it is an apocalypse, end of days and a precursor to the return of the Messiah and the day of the Lord. Enoch's warnings are not conditional, but rather a warning of what is going to happen, no matter what (Enoch 1:9, 9:3, 47:1, 61:4). The book of Revelation is more encouraging with the emphasis on the possibility of enduring to the end, therefore more pastoral and not as fatalistic.

The book of Enoch's strength is how it informs us on the topic of Angelology. Ephesians chapter 6 specifically throws out some interesting key words of rulers, authorities, cosmic powers and spiritual forces of evil in the heavenly realms. Scholars in the past have all really thrown these classifications into the word 'demon'. If we specifically look at the word 'rulers', it is used in Enoch and Daniel. This description is also in 1st Corinthians 2 and Enoch deals with it in a more broad sense. The book of Daniel is largely influenced by this idea of geographical rulers ie: 'Prince of Persia', lending itself heavily to the world view of Deuteronomy 32 and Psalms 82, whereby the nations were given up to these rulers as a form of judgement, meaning that chaos was sown among the nations (Heiser, The Unseen Realm 329-330). Geographical rulers stood in enmity toward God and instead of serving their purpose as the 'Angelic Host', decided that they enjoyed being worshipped themselves and went rogue. This is largely where the apostle Paul gets these descriptions. Naturally, just because the apostle Paul may be allegedly borrowing from the Enochian world view, does not necessarily mean that he is suggesting that the book of Enoch should be part of the inspired canon.

The way Enoch starts to move away from what we would consider as Orthodox Christian belief, is linked to the parables in the book of Enoch and the dependency of salvation by works (1 Enoch 37-44). This is however fully in keeping with the Old Covenant, as there is no reliance on the finished works of the Messiah. The righteous are, therefore, judged based on their devotion to the law, whereas the unrighteousness are judged based on their general level of wickedness. There is a recurrent theme of the abuse of power in Enoch and the need for social justice.

The reason why the book of Enoch becomes such a point of interest for Angelology, is that it introduces the context of 'the watchers', to the confusing passages in Genesis 6. The account of the Book of Enoch will be forever associated with the increased corruption on earth in Genesis 6:1-4, referring to the 'Sons of God' rather than the 'Watchers':

'When man began to multiply on the face of the land and daughters were born to them, ² the **sons of God** *saw that the daughters of man were attractive. And they took as their wives any they chose. ³ Then the LORD said, "My Spirit shall not abide in[a] man forever, for he is flesh: his days shall be 120 years." ⁴ The Nephilim[b] were on the earth in those days, and also afterward, when the* **sons of God** *came in to the daughters of man and they bore children to them. These were the mighty men who were of old, the men of renown'.* **Genesis 6:1-4**

It thus also becomes a very good explanation point to the key question that troubles most believers and non believers alike, and that is on the 'origin of good and evil'. Many of the references in Enoch serve as a useful way to fill in the gaps to explain the level of depravity man fell into following the first fall in the Garden of Eden and the second fall in Genesis 6. The interesting aspect about this book is that it also uses names of members of the 'Angelic Host' that left their abode and engaged in activities beyond their remit. As mentioned before, the only named Angels in the protestant canon are Michael and Gabriel, with the addition of Raphael in the Catholic apocrypha.

Many more angels or 'Watchers' are listed and named specifically in the books of Enoch. I have devoted my attention mainly to the first book of Enoch, as it deals specifically with the fall of the Watchers. The second book of Enoch is shrouded in more mystery and controversy and deals with the 5th heaven where the decision of the Fall takes place. The third book of Enoch gives us more detail as to the 'Watchers' that did not leave their abode, therefore remaining in an unfallen state. The Fallen traditionally were viewed to have been 200, whereby the leaders of these numbers are the only ones to have been named. We also have a list of the archangels including Raphael who under the instructions of God chained them until the appointed time (1 Enoch 22:6).

The events of this fall are briefly summarized as a number of angels or 'Watchers' having been given a task to watch over humanity. As previously described, they begin to desire the women there and by the prompting of their leader Samyaza, take for themselves human wives and completely according to their own volition, instruct men in skills and arts previously unknown to them. They procreate with human women, who give birth to ravaging giants and with their instruction of forbidden knowledge, sow chaos amongst humanity. They taught their new students technologies such as weaponry, cosmetics, mirrors, sorcery and other dark arts. The parallel with Genesis 6 using the term 'Sons of God', and Enoch using the term 'Watchers', is undeniable. Eventually we see God bring the flood in both Genesis and Enoch to rid the earth of the evil that has been sown and the flesh which has been so corrupted.

The book of Enoch names an angel called Uriel who is tasked to instruct Noah to prevent the complete eradication of the human race. The Fallen Watchers from that moment on were bound in a place called the 'Valley of the Earth', which is confirmed by Jude 6.

The Leadership of these rogue Watchers listed in the book of Enoch are documented as having been in charge of certain groups.

1. Shemihazah, their leader;
2. Arteqoph, second to him;
3. Remashel, third to him;
4. Kokabel, fourth to him;
5. Armumahel, fifth to him;
6. Ramel, sixth to him;
7. Daniel, seventh to him;
8. Ziqel, eighth to him;
9. Baraqel, ninth to him;
10. Asael, tenth to him;
11. Hermani, eleventh to him;
12. Matarel, twelfth to him;
13. Ananel, thirteenth to him;
14. Setawel, fourteenth to him;
15. Samshiel, fifteenth to him;
16. Sahriel, sixteenth to him;
17. Tummiel, seventeenth to him;
18. Turiel, eighteenth to him;
19. Yamiel, nineteenth to him;
20. Yehadiel, twentieth to him.
(Nickelsburg, 2004)

Enoch lists specific leaders among the fallen angels who engaged in sexual union with women. Many of these are also listed in the books including the Zohar and the book of Jubilees. What they were charged with is listed as the following:

- Araqiel taught humans the signs of the earth.
- Armaros in Enoch I taught humanity the resolving of enchantments.
- Azazel taught humans to make knives, swords, shields, and how to devise ornaments and cosmetics.
- Gadreel taught the art of cosmetics, the use of weapons and killing blows.
- Baraqel taught astrology.

- Bezaliel mentioned in Enoch I is left out of most translations because of damaged manuscripts and problematic transmission of the text.
- Chazaqiel taught humans the signs of the clouds (meteorology).
- Kokabiel in Enoch I, is a fallen watcher, resident of the nether realms, and commands 365,000 surrogate spirits to do his bidding. Among other duties, he instructs his fellows in astrology.
- Penemue "taught mankind the art of writing with ink and paper," and taught "the children of men the bitter and the sweet and the secrets of wisdom." (I Enoch 69.8)
- Sariel taught humankind about the courses of the moon.
- Samyaza is one of the leaders of the fall from heaven.
- Shamsiel, once a guardian of Eden as stated in the *Zohar*, served as one of the two chief aides to the archangel Uriel. In *Jubilees*, he is referred to as one of the Watchers. He is a fallen angel who teaches the signs of the sun.
- Yeqon was the ringleader who first tempted the other Watchers into having sexual relations with humans. His accomplices were Asbeel, Gadreel, Penemue, and Kasdaye (or Kasadya), who were all identified as individual "satans".

If you have ever wondered, where and how humanity managed to gain certain knowledge from virtual cave man existence to the technological brilliance of the building of the pyramids, this may indeed answer a lot of unanswered questions. It may also point us in the right direction as to why God may have felt it necessary to press the reboot button in view of the increased levels of depravity amongst men. It is particularly Azazel who seems to carry a lot of the pressure of blame as he was the one who taught humanity how to make swords and knives, and shields, and breastplates, teaching them about all the metals of the earth and the art of working them including all the workings of vanity (Enoch VIII). The devastation that then followed was witnessed from above by Michael, Gabriel, Suriel and Uriel and Chapter 9 makes it clear that they were not impressed; so much so that they petitioned the Lord as to what action they should take against the rogue watchers. With all quotations from Enoch 1, parallel quotations showing similarities in language and events from the accepted canon and second temple literature have been included.

1 And then Michael, Gabriel, Suriel and Uriel, looked down from Heaven and saw the mass of blood that was being shed on the earth and all the iniquity that was being done on the earth. (Genesis 6:11-12), (Jeremiah 23:10), (Job 9:24), (Psalm 107:34), (Hosea 1:2), (Jeremiah 3:9), (Hosea 4:1-2), (Genesis 6:5-6)

2 And they said to one another: "Let the devastated Earth cry out with the sound of their cries, up to the Gate of Heaven.

3 And now to you, Oh Holy Ones of Heaven, the souls of men complain, saying: "Bring our complaint before the Most High."

4 And they said to their Lord, the King: "Lord of Lords, God of Gods, King of Kings! Your glorious throne endures for all the generations of the world, and blessed and praised! (Deuteronomy 10:17), (1 Timothy 6:14-16), (Psalm 83:18), (Ephesians 4:6), (Isaiah 66:1), (Ben Sira 1:8-9), (Acts 7:49), (1 Chronicles 29:10-12)

5 You have made everything, and power over everything is yours. And everything is uncovered, and open, in front of you, and you see everything, and there is nothing that can be hidden from you. (Hebrews 4:13), (Psalm 139:1-4), (1 Samuel 2:3), (Luke 12:30), (Matthew 6:7-8), (1 John 3:20), (Romans 11:33-36), (Job 34:21-22), (Job 42:1-2), (Psalm 38:9)

6 See then what Azazel has done; how he has taught all iniquity on the earth and revealed the eternal secrets that are made in Heaven.

7 And Semyaza has made known spells, he to whom you gave authority to rule over those who are with him.

8 And they went into the daughters of men together, lay with those women, became unclean, and revealed to them these sins. (Genesis 6:1-2), (Genesis 6:4-5), (Genesis 6:11), (Numbers 13:33).

9 And the women bore giants, and thereby the whole Earth has been filled with blood and iniquity. (Genesis 6:1-2), (Genesis 6:4-5), (Genesis 6:11), (Numbers 13:33).

10 And now behold the souls which have died cry out and complain unto the Gate of Heaven, and their lament has ascended, and they cannot go out in the face of the iniquity which is being committed on the earth. (Revelation 6:10)

11 And you know everything, before it happens, and you know this, and what concerns each of them. But you say nothing to us. What ought we to do with them, about this?" (Isaiah 45:11), (Isaiah 46:9-10), (Isaiah 48:4-6), (Luke 8:17), (Mark 4:22), (Matthew 10:26), (Luke 12:2-3), (Job 24:1) **Enoch 9: 1-11**

In chapter 10 of Enoch 1, God replies in a manner of taking swift action against the rogue Watchers. Furthermore, it is evidently clear that redemption is not available to these entities who failed in the responsibility they had been given and used it to their own ends. Although the Watchers seem to repent of their actions, their petition for forgiveness is denied. The archangel Raphael is given the responsibility to bind Azazel hand and foot and imprison him until the appointed time of judgement. The archangel Gabriel was tasked with bringing destruction upon the offspring of the watchers so they would turn on one another and thereby destroy each other, even before the arrival of the great flood. The archangel Michael was instructed to inform Semyaza and his followers of his fate: furthermore, watch the destruction of their offspring and then to suffer the same imprisonment until the appointed hour of judgement and eternal torment:

Enoch Chapter 10

1 And then the Most High, the Great and Holy One, spoke and sent Arsyalalyur to the son of Lamech, and said to him:

2 "Say to him in my name; hide yourself! And reveal to him the end, which is coming, because the whole earth will be destroyed. A deluge is about to come on all the earth; and all that is in it will be destroyed. (Genesis 6:8), (Ben Sira 44:17-18), (Genesis 6:17), (Genesis 7:6-24), (2 Peter 3:6), (Luke 17:27), (Hebrews 11:7).

3 And now teach him so that he may escape and his offspring may survive for the whole Earth." (Ben Sira 44:17-18), (Proverbs 10:16), (Proverbs 11:19), (Proverbs 14:27), (Genesis 7:1, 6-7, 13), (Genesis 9:1), (Genesis 9:7), (Genesis 9:18-19), (Genesis 10:1, 32), (Wisdom 14:6)

4 And further the Lord said to Raphael: "Bind Azazel by his hands and his feet and throw him into the darkness. And split open the desert, which is in Dudael, and throw him there.

5 And throw on him jagged and sharp stones and cover him with darkness. And let him stay there forever. And cover his face so that he may not see the light.

6 And so that, on the Great Day of Judgment, he may be hurled into the fire. (Isaiah 24:21-22), (2 Peter 2:4), (Jude 1:6), (Revelation 20:1-3)

7 And restore the Earth which the Angels have ruined. And announce the restoration of the Earth. For I shall restore the Earth so that not all the sons of men shall be destroyed because of the knowledge which the Watchers made known and taught to their sons. (Joel 2:22)

8 And the whole Earth has been ruined by the teaching of the works of Azazel; and against him write: ALL SIN." (Genesis 6:5-7), (Genesis 6:12)

9 And the Lord said to Gabriel: "Proceed against the bastards, and the reprobates, and against the sons of the fornicators. And destroy the sons of the fornicators, and the sons of the Watchers, from amongst men. And send them out, and send them against one another, and let them destroy themselves in battle; for they will not have length of days. (Baruch 3:24-28), (Wisdom 14:6)

10 And they will petition you, but the petitioners will gain nothing in respect of them, for they hope for eternal life, and that each of them will live life for five hundred years."

11 And the Lord said to Michael: "Go, inform Semyaza, and the others with him, who have associated with the women to corrupt themselves with them in all their uncleanness.

12 When all their sons kill each other, and when they see the destruction of their loved ones, bind them for seventy generations, under the hills of the earth, until the day of their judgment and of their consummation, until the judgment, which is for all eternity, is accomplished. (2 Peter 2:4, (Jude 1:6)

13 And in those days, they will lead them to the Abyss of Fire; in torment, and in prison they will be shut up for all eternity. (Psalm 140:10), (Revelation 19:20), (Revelation 20:10)

14 And then Semyaza will be burnt, and from then on destroyed with them; together they will be bound until the end of all generations. (Revelation 20:15), (Psalm 68:2), (Psalm 73:27)

15 And destroy all the souls of lust, and the sons of the Watchers, for they have wronged men. (Baruch 3:24-28)

16 Destroy all wrong from the face of the Earth and every evil work will cease. (Isaiah 60:21-22)

17 And now all the righteous will be humble, and will live until they beget thousands. And all the days of their youth, and their sabbaths, they will fulfill in peace. (Exodus 20:6; Deuteronomy 5:10), (Isaiah 61:3)

18 And in those days the whole earth will be tilled in righteousness and all of it will be planted with trees; and it will be filled with blessing. (Exodus 20:6; Deuteronomy 5:10), (Isaiah 61:3)

19 And all the pleasant trees they will plant on it and they will plant on it vines. And the vine that is planted on it will produce fruit in abundance; and every seed that is sown on it, each measure will produce a thousand, and each measure of olives will produce ten baths of oil.

20 And you cleanse the Earth from all wrong, and from all iniquity, and from all sin, and from all impiety, and from all the uncleanness which is brought about on the earth. (2 Peter 2:17-18), (Jude 1:12-15)

21 And all the sons of men shall be righteous, and all the nations shall serve and bless me and all shall worship me. (Psalm 72:11), (Psalm 86:9)

22 And the Earth will be cleansed from all corruption, and from all sin, and from all wrath, and from all torment; and I will not again send a flood upon it, for all generations, forever. (Revelation 21:4)

The classification of the Holy Angels who watch (some of whom are high ranking angels in the accepted protestant canon) including their job descriptions are given in Enoch chapter 20 as the following:

1. 'And these are the names of the holy angels who watch. (Revelation 8:2), (Hebrews 1:7), (Revelation 1:4), (Revelation 4:5), (Revelation 5:6), (Zechariah 4:10) (Revelation 1:16), (Revelation 1:20), (Zechariah 3:9), (Revelation 2:1), (Revelation 3:1), (Revelation 15:6)

2. Uriel, one of the holy angels, who is over the world and over Tartarus.

3. Raphael, one of the holy angels, who is over the spirits of men. (Tobías 12:15), (Tobías 3:16-17), (Tobías 5:4-17), (Tobías 6), (Tobías 12:15-22)

4. Raguel, one of the holy angels who takes vengeance on the world of the luminaries.

5. Michael, one of the holy angels, to wit, he that is set over the best part of mankind and over chaos. (Daniel 10:13), (Daniel 10:21), (Daniel 12:1), (Jude 1:9), (Revelation 12:7)

6. Saraqael, one of the holy angels, who is set over the spirits, who sin in the spirit.

7.Gabriel, one of the holy angels, who is over Paradise and the serpents and the Cherubim. (Daniel 8:16), (Daniel 9:21), (Luke 1:19), (Luke 1:26), (Genesis 3:24), (Exodus 25:18-22), (Ezekiel 10:4-5)

8. Remiel, one of the holy angels, whom God set over those who rise'. **Enoch 20:1-8**

In conclusion, Enoch 1 is an important piece of literature, because the authors of the Bible were familiar with it, although not referencing it word for word, it is clear that they quoted events from it in both Testaments and wrote in a way to incorporate the Enochian worldview. Jude even mentions Enoch by name. Historically, this is the lens in which the Jewish world viewed the topic of angelology. The book of Enoch does not contradict scripture and serves as useful material on the origin of demons and the Nephilim. It adds further reasoning as to why many of the angels fell from heaven: furthermore, serves as a useful ancient source to determine extra names of the angelic host. When viewing the pressing question of good and evil, it serves as a very good explanation as to why it became morally necessary for God to put into motion the flood in Genesis. The added context of the Enochian history also serves as another moral explanation as to why God instructed Joshua to wipe out all the tribes in Canaan who were also descendants of Giants (human hybrids). This was a clear move to wipe out the seed of sin and further source of corruption in the world. The book of Enoch also serves as a prophetic exposition of the age of peace characterized by the Messianic age.

Learning Points

- *The book of Enoch 1 is Second Temple Literature.*
- *The book of Enoch is relevant as the New Testament writers were fully aware of the content of Enoch.*
- *Enoch is not considered to be the inspired Word of God, but a book does not have to be in the Bible to be theologically relevant.*

- *The Qumran sect held the book of Enoch as sacred and included it in the Dead Sea Scrolls.*
- *Had Enoch have been written in Hebrew, it would have warranted more validity.*
- *Enoch is an apocalyptic book.*
- *The fall of the 'Watchers', is the contextual account of Genesis 6 in an Enochian view of that event.*
- *The books of Jude, 2ⁿᵈ Peter and Revelation have clear distinctions of Enochian scripting. Jude mentions Enoch by name.*
- *The 'Watchers', are linked to the authors of evil.*
- *Enoch informs us about angelology in detail and lists many more names of angels and watchers.*
- *Enoch lends itself heavily to the Deuteronomy 32 and Psalm 82 worldview concerning fallen angels as geographical rulers and principalities.*
- *Enoch uses the term 'Watchers', instead of 'Sons of God'.*
- *Enoch is a good source informing us about the origin of evil and the passing on of forbidden knowledge and dark arts.*
- *There is no instance where the book of Enoch contradicts scripture in the accepted canon.*
- *The accounts in Enoch serve as a good reason why God had to bring about a global flood to wipe out the corruption of all flesh and why he instructed Joshua to destroy all the tribes in Canaan.*

MISCONCEPTIONS ABOUT ANGELS

The mesmerizing topic of angels has been a fixation for many over the ages. Therefore, it comes as no surprise that a number of misconceptions would accompany these objects of fascination. The sources of misconceptions for the most part are largely due to a lack of grounding in academia. Many Bible translations do not even require a Christian translator. Furthermore, the generalization of the term can largely be due to linguistics. There has been little time attributed to ancient sources for the purpose of the context of biblical sources or the use of second temple literature to gain an understanding of Jewish thought during the time of the writing of primary sources. A lot of information we have gleaned in angelology has relied on the imagination of artists and their depictions of heavenly beings in mosaics, tapestry, stain glass windows and paintings.

One of the most common misconceptions is that angels have wings. There is absolutely no reference anywhere in scripture pertaining to that imagination. Just because a heavenly being can fly, ascend and descend does not mean that it requires the law of physics in operation to do so. We don't depict the ascension of Jesus with the growth of wings to ascend to the Father. The only biblical examples of spiritual beings having wings are in the case of Cherubim and Seraphim, and technically, these are not angels. They are not used to deliver a 'message' (malach). The terminology of Cherubim and Seraphim are fixed in scripture and do not go beyond their function and are thereby not substituted for each other. The role Cherubim and Seraphim play is to guard the throne of God and his holiness. Their function is to keep watch over sacred space, not to fly to earth and instruct humanity on the plan of God. They also do not appear in full human form, but are likened to majestic creatures considered to be fierce in the animal kingdom.

Amongst all the evidence I have brought forward, it is clear that when angels appear to people, they do so in human form, which includes both testaments. The terms 'in appearance of a man', are quite telling. Whether this is their actual form has not been revealed to us. New Testament examples make this so obvious, as we are led to believe by the writer of Hebrews, that we indeed may have entertained angels without even knowing it. This is in keeping with making sacrifices in life to please God:

'Let brotherly love continue. [2] Do not neglect to show hospitality to strangers, for thereby some have entertained angels unawares'. **Hebrews 13:1-2**

Another example that shows us that humans are frequently indistinguishable from angels is when the church community was worried about the apostle Peter, as James had already been killed by the sword under the instruction of Herod. Peter was arrested and imprisoned and guarded by four squads of soldiers. Peter was woken by the angel and literally had no idea if he was experiencing a vision or not. All he did know, is that his shackles dropped off him, he was told to put on his sandals and the angel guided him passed the four squads of soldiers, some of whom he had previously been shackled to. The most interesting part is when the servant girl who recognized the voice of Peter was made fun of by the community as they explained to her, that it is likely to have been his angel standing at the door. This goes to show that they were used to spiritual beings in human form or 'likeness of a man' dwelling amongst them:

'Now when Herod was about to bring him out, on that very night, Peter was sleeping between two soldiers, bound with two chains, and sentries before the door were guarding the prison. ⁷And behold, an angel of the Lord stood next to him, and a light shone in the cell. He struck Peter on the side and woke him, saying, "Get up quickly." And the chains fell off his hands. ⁸And the angel said to him, "Dress yourself and put on your sandals." And he did so. And he said to him, "Wrap your cloak around you and follow me." ⁹And he went out and followed him. He did not know that what was being done by the angel was real, but thought he was seeing a vision. ¹⁰When they had passed the first and the second guard, they came to the iron gate leading into the city. It opened for them of its own accord, and they went out and went along one street, and immediately the angel left him. ¹¹When Peter came to himself, he said, "Now I am sure that the Lord has sent his angel and rescued me from the hand of Herod and from all that the Jewish people were expecting."

¹²When he realized this, he went to the house of Mary, the mother of John whose other name was Mark, where many were gathered together and were praying. ¹³And when he knocked at the door of the gateway, a servant girl named Rhoda came to answer. ¹⁴Recognizing Peter's voice, in her joy she did not open the gate but ran in and reported that Peter was standing at the gate. ¹⁵They said to her, "You are out of your mind." But she kept insisting that it was so, and they kept saying, **"It is his angel!"** *¹⁶But Peter continued knocking, and when they opened, they saw him and were* *amazed.* *[17]* *But motioning to them with his hand to be silent, he described to them how the Lord had brought him out of the prison. And he said, "Tell these things to James and to the brothers."[a] Then he departed and went to another place'.* **Acts 12: 6 -17**

When we consider evidence from scripture concerning the appearance of angels, it is clear that the only time they become recognisable from an ordinary human, is if their appearance shines like lightning (Matt 28:3), or if they do something which is clearly evidence of God intervening in the natural realm.

The next obvious question in relation to this is that of gender. Angels are spirit beings and gender is a biological attribute. Angels are in fact genderless, but do not manifest themselves in scripture in the appearance of a woman. (The Genesis 6 account, however, only takes place due to the fact of disobedient 'Sons of God', leaving their *natural habitation* and remit, choosing to become embodied). They have always been described as men. In the case of Sodom and Gomorrah they were clearly worth a second look. Some people try and suggest that Zechariah chapter 5, pertains to women with wings of a stork, lifting up a basket between heaven and earth, but we do not have an indication that these are actually angels. In the book of Zechariah 5:10, when an angel speaks, it uses the masculine form of the verb, not the feminine. The women with baskets were a symbol of the removal of evil from the Land and the people of Babylon which is the residing place of all evil (Heiser, 2018).

We always need to return to the notion, that 'angels', take on physical form when appearing to man. A messenger is a job description, and taking on physical form in the appearance of a man helps with getting this job done. Most people especially with Daniel and Zechariah were quite startled, but this adds to the mystery. The other thing we need to consider is that when angels are sent, they are not always sent in physical form. At the beginning of this book we discovered that a spirit from the

'Divine Council' was sent to confuse the mouth of the prophets in order to bring an end to the rule of the unrighteous King Ahab (2 Kings 22: 20-22). The spirit that stood before the Lord to volunteer for this method of approach received permission to accomplish the task, but was not embodied ie: the spirit did not appear in physical form.

On the topic of angels, there is this assumption that when the epic war took place in the heavenlies, one third of the angels fell with the adversary, which leaves two thirds of angels with the blessed Trinity to restore God's plan. Unfortunately, we do not have any evidence of this in scripture. We know that the adversary fell from heaven, but we have no reference of a third of the angelic host following him. Revelation chapters 9 and 10 are very characteristic of this, and stars or luminaries were frequently used to describe angels, but there is no indication as to the number joining the rebellion.

9 'And the great dragon was thrown down, that ancient serpent, who is called the devil and Satan, the deceiver of the whole world—he was thrown down to the earth, and his angels were thrown down with him'. **Revelation 12:9**

On the topic of rebellion, there also seems to be this idea that angels themselves are now set in a fixed place of obedience. We do not specifically get this indication from scripture. It is clear from the whole story that unfolds in the Bible that God's 'Holy Ones', are not perfect or beyond falling. The book of Job gives us more clarity on this issue and forces us to look at the 'Divine Council' as not without error:

'Behold, God[a] puts no trust in his holy ones,
 and the heavens are not pure in his sight'. **Job 15:15**

'Can mortal man be in the right before[a] God?
 Can a man be pure before his Maker?

¹⁸Even in his servants he puts no trust,
  *and his angels he charges with error; **Job 4:17-18***

Although the book of Job is traditionally put on the same time line as the book of Genesis, it is clear that these events are well after the initial fall in the garden of Eden. God puts no trust in his 'Holy Ones' and he charges his angels with error. God is omniscient and is well ahead of the game. Whether they are immortal or eternal, naturally rests upon God's will. They are created beings, so therefore had a beginning. Their end rests with the decisions of the Almighty. In view of the Genesis 6 scenario with the added context of second temple literature, the apostle Paul alludes to something very interesting in regard to 1. Male authority 2. Angelic implication:

'Therefore the woman ought to have a sign of authority on her head, for the sake of the angels [so as not to offend them]'. ***1 Corinthians 11:10***

Some view this verse as Paul hinting at the possibility of history repeating itself, as the angels are always watching. It is likely however, that this verse is more in line with symbols of marriage and spiritual headship in the home.

Concerning life after death, one of the popular beliefs about angels is that they take a person to heaven when they die. This is very much in line with wanting to comfort people due to a loss or tragedy: furthermore, a way to instill hope in a person slipping away. One of the most quoted sources for this is naturally the story of the 'Rich man and Lazarus', which was an account taught by Jesus. Many people for some reason decide that it was a parable, but we have no evidence to suggest that Jesus was not giving an example of the actual workings of life after death. In this account, the rich man faces a place of torment and Lazarus is taken to a place called 'Abraham's bosom', characterized as paradise in the afterlife. This is often seen as the good side of Sheol.

22 'The poor man died and was carried by the angels to Abraham's side.[a] The rich man also died and was buried'. **Luke 16:22**

As pointed out earlier in this book, the image of angels escorting people to heaven is common both in the Bible and second temple literature including the pseudepigrapha. The archangel Michael disputing with the adversary concerning the body of Moses also helps to impress this image in our thinking (Jude 1:9). In the case of Abraham, 'The Testament of Abraham', (20:10-12) tells of the account of the archangel Michael, bearing his precious soul in his hands. If we look at other apocryphal sources such as the 'Testament of Job' we also see this common theme, as Job falls ill. After a number of days of illness he was able to see those who were coming for his soul. A chariot arrives and he is greeted by the driver and taking his soul he flies up to the east, whilst the body is prepared for burial (Testament of Job 52: 1-12). There is no reason to suggest that angels are not a part of escorting a soul into the afterlife, as Jesus himself gives us this example in Luke. Therefore, the second temple literature regarding Job and Abraham may have some truth in them.

This also puts a clear line in between the concept of humanity and angels. Both these terms are also not interchangeable. A human does not become an angel after death. We will in time receive a resurrection body like Christ (1 Cor 15:35-38), but there is no scriptural evidence to suggest that we become 'messengers', or spirits working on behalf of God to intervene in the natural realm. Just because man has a soul and a spirit, does not mean that we become ministering spirits. A matter of fact, we will no longer be a little lower than the angels as far as altitude is concerned (Heb 2:7), but we will indeed rule with Christ if we persist (*2 Timothy 2:12).* We shall be like him (1 John 3:2). We will be placed in positions of rule, and replacing the entities known as the 'Fallen sons of God', and sharing the messianic rule with Jesus (Hebrews 2:5-18). This means that in the new Eden we will be above the angels.

A common theme I have observed over the years, particularly in charismatic evangelical circles is the belief that Christians have been given the authority by God to command angels to do their bidding. I have yet to come across any scriptural evidence to suggest this is possible or encouraged. This idea comes from Hebrews 1:13-14

¹³ 'And to which of the angels has he ever said,

"Sit at my right hand
 until I make your enemies a footstool for your feet"?

¹⁴ Are they not all ministering spirits sent out to serve for the sake of those who are to inherit salvation'? **Hebrews 1:13-14**

The first thing we need to realize about this verse, is that it is in a cluster of verses in chapter 1 speaking of the supremacy of Christ. The only time believers feature in these verses pertains to those who are to inherit salvation. We may indeed one day after we have run the race and passed the test in this life, go into the next and become a part of the judging process of angels:

³ 'Do you not know that we are to judge angels? How much more, then, matters pertaining to this life'! **1 Corinthians 6:3**

To put this verse into context, if we read the whole of chapter 6, the example of judging angels was used to encourage believers to judge correctly according to God's law when dealing with disputes. Paul was not happy with believers taking trivial cases to secular courts amongst believers. In the same chapter this also pertains to believers one day judging the world. In this life, although we are to test the spirits, we do not have authority to project them around the place to get what we want:

'Beloved, do not believe every spirit, but test the spirits to see whether they are from God, for many false prophets have gone out into the world. ²By this you know the Spirit of God: every spirit that confesses that Jesus Christ has come in the flesh is from God, ³ and every spirit that does not confess Jesus is not from God. This is the spirit of the antichrist, which you heard was coming and now is in the world already. ⁴Little children, you are from God and have overcome them, for he who is in you is greater than he who is in the world. ⁵They are from the world; therefore they speak from the world, and the world listens to them. ⁶We are from God. Whoever knows God listens to us; whoever is not from God does not listen to us. By this we know the Spirit of truth and the spirit of error'. 1 John 4:1-6

When reviewing Hebrews 1:14, it interprets angels as ministering spirits sent out to serve those who inherit salvation; it is only meant for them to assist believers during their life as a believer. There is a big difference between the concept of 'sent to serve' and 'authority to command'. Furthermore, we do not have a single example in scripture when a human used their own authority, fulfilling their own needs, by telling an angel what to do. When humans have had angelic encounters, they are mostly startled, thought they were dreaming and asked a lot of questions. They did not tell the angel what to do or give them a task to fulfill. This is not Christian practice and is rooted more in the 'new age', taking up contact with one's guardian angel, or unlocking their power. A matter of fact, we are not encouraged to look for angels at all. They are what their name suggests; 'messengers' and spiritual beings that work on behalf of God intervening in the natural realm either in word or in deed. Communion with spirits other than the Holy Spirit is expressly forbidden and in many cases is more reminiscent of witchcraft and the need for following a spirit guide. This is the adversary's oldest trick in the book as he was the deceiver in the beginning:

*¹⁴ And no wonder, for even **Satan disguises himself as an angel of light.** ¹⁵ So it is no surprise if his servants, also, disguise themselves* *as servants of righteousness. Their end will correspond to their deeds'.* **2 Corinthians 11: 14-15**

If we take the example of Revelation 19:9-10, when John receives the vision of the marriage supper with the lamb, the angel puts the topic of devotion in the necessary order and context:

*⁹And the angel said[a] to me, "Write this: Blessed are those who are invited to the marriage supper of the Lamb." And he said to me, "These are the true words of God." ¹⁰ **Then I fell down at his feet to worship him, but he said to me, "You must not do that! I am a fellow servant with you and your brothers who hold to the testimony of Jesus.** Worship God." For the testimony of Jesus is the spirit of prophecy'. (Revelation 19:9-10)*

As believers imitating Christ is what all of us are called to do. Jesus broke things down to us gradually, step by step including teaching us the Lord's Prayer. When we look at His response in the garden of Gethsemane during Jesus' betrayal and arrest, we see the image of the suffering servant. The Saviour who is laying down his life as a ransom for many. The language Jesus uses upon Peter defending him with a sword is as follows:

⁵³'Do you think that I cannot appeal to my Father, and he will at once send me more than twelve legions of angels'? **Matthew 26:53**

He had sought the Father's will, even to the point of not letting the cup of suffering pass him by, yet he lets everyone know, that could have 'appealed to the Father' to set him free with twelve legions of angels. He did not say that he would simply command them to do so, although previously he could calm the storm and the elements of nature. The key here, is asking the Father for angelic intervention. This is something we can do. However, commanding them to do what we want is not evidential in scripture. Jesus had the authority to do so, yet he modelled what we are meant to emulate as believers.

If you are fixated with the topic of angels, then seek the 'Angel of the Lord', who is no one else than Jesus himself. The Angel of the LORD encamps around those who fear him, and delivers them (Psalm 34:7). If you require the ministry of angels in your life, then there is one safe way to enhance their engagement, and that it is in the form of a frequent and faith-filled prayer life. The angel Gabriel was immediately dispatched after Daniel prayed (Daniel 9:23). In the case of Peter in Acts, when the church was praying for him, an angel was sent to set him free from prison. It is evidently clear from scripture, that prayer and being in communion with Christ enhances angelic intervention. The only revealed names of angels in the most reliable canon are, 'Gabriel' meaning 'God is my power', and 'Michael' means 'Who is like God?'. Both these names in their very nature only give glory to God.

Learning Points

- *Our knowledge of angelology has largely been reliant on the imagination of artists and their depictions of heavenly beings in mosaics, tapestry, stain glass windows and paintings; not on primary sources or academia.*
- *Angels contrary to popular mythology do not have wings. Cherubim and Seraphim do have wings.*
- *Angels according to scripture manifest in appearance of men, not as women. There are no examples of angels manifesting in appearance of a woman.*
- *Humans can in some cases be indistinguishable from angels e.g (Acts 12).*
- *Peter's angel may not have been unlike Peter in appearance (Acts 12).*
- *Many have entertained angels unaware (Hebrews 13).*
- *Angels intervene in the natural world to save human beings from harm and in some cases pass deadly judgement on the wicked in accordance with the will of God. eg (Exodus 12:29-32)(2 Kings 19:35)(Acts 12:23).*

- *When angels manifest, they can do so in the appearance of men, but also shine as bright as lightning, with clothes as white as snow (Matthew 28:3).*
- *Angels can fulfill their mission as spirits in disembodied form (2 Kings 22:20-22) , or accomplish their assignment in embodied form.*
- *There is no evidence in scripture that one third of the angelic host fell with the adversary. This is tradition, but not evidence based.*
- *Angels have free will and are not beyond falling, and if they do are beyond redemption.*
- *There is scriptural evidence to suggest that angels can take people to heaven.*
- *Humans are human, angels are angels. Humans do not become angels after death. The redeemed have a higher calling.*
- *The redeemed will share a messianic rule with Jesus.*
- *Believers have not been given the authority to command their own personal angel to do their bidding. Christians are required to pray to God and He may release angels according to His will and purpose. We are discouraged from taking up communication with spirits in scripture.*
- *Jesus could appeal to the Father to send legions of angels, but did not command them verbally in scripture.*

SUMMARY

As we began our Biblical journey analyzing the concept of the 'Angelic Host', the first thing we considered was the continued story unfolding between man and God. The other characters portrayed in scripture aided our understanding of the spirit realm including angels (embodied or disembodied spirits), archangel(s), cherubim, seraphim, principalities and powers (some of which imprisoned awaiting judgement), the adversary and demons (low-level spirits). They are cast as spiritual beings (elohim) that inhabit the realm of the heavens, overlapping with our earthly dimension.

These spiritual beings have their own characteristics and the authors of the Bible used specific key words to define all the inhabitants of the spiritual realm. Old Testament Hebrew uses the word: 'elohim', whereas the New Testament Greek uses the word: 'theos'. The difficulty in gaining an overall picture, is assessing which word is being referred to. This depends on the use of capital letters and context, which requires someone in the knowhow to determine who is being referred to in the spiritual realm, whether 'God', or another spiritual being.

'Elohim', is therefore not a specific name, but a title. The word 'elohim', can be both singular or plural. A big term of respect in Hebrew was the term 'Yahweh', for God, being the name revealed to Moses. Titles, however, also included the key word 'elohim', which was defined as a category, with full knowledge of who they were referring to. 'There is no Elohim beside 'Yahweh', indicated that there was none by comparison as he was seen as Creator God.

Christianity and Judaism are of course Monotheistic Religions; therefore, the Biblical writers are clear in their communication, that there is only one spiritual being out there who is the Prime Mover and Creator of all things including the key term 'elohim'. This is at the exclusion of other spiritual rulers with the same title. Monotheism found in scripture communicates that one specific Elohim 'Yahweh', is above all other elohim, meaning other spiritual beings in the heavenly realm. Elohim in scripture is a term used as either 'God', or other 'spiritual beings'. There are a number of elohim in scripture that have a number of titles including 'Host of Heaven', 'Sons of God', 'Holy Ones', 'Heavenly Ones', and 'Divine Council' (Heiser, Unseen Realm, 2015).

Looking at all cultures of the past, there is no escaping the fact that wherever one finds oneself in the world, there is a belief in the spiritual realm, mirroring the life in the natural. This is of course the same in Judeo-Christian thinking, not just a process resembling, but also overlapping realms. Scripture highlights the difference of earthly with divine, by defining God's space as the sky or heavens, as what is seen above can be viewed as timeless and eternal. We may see the stars as simple luminaries, but the authors of the Bible likened them to spiritual beings and used the mystery behind them to communicate their nature. Scripture calls them 'The Sons of God', 'Rulers and Authorities', and in certain instances 'The Divine Council'. The study of these terms and application to theology have been largely overlooked in applied Christian thinking. We see the introduction to the 'Divine Council' in the first book of Genesis when they are referred to as 'Hosts of Heaven'. The sun, moon and stars. Here they are seen as signs of power and stature, signs pointing to the ultimate status in the universe and God's omnipotence. They are appointed to rule over the day and night. They celebrated with joy when God used his unlimited creativity to create the world (Job 38:7).

Church history has largely ignored the existence of other spiritual beings in the heavenlies and we have always used a general term of 'angel', being a 'messenger' accomplishing a divine mission or relaying an important message. Could it be, however, that there are indeed other spiritual beings in conversation with God, joining in the decision-making on earth like a spiritual staff team? This is not a reflection on God's omniscience neither his omnipotence, but he clearly enjoys sharing decision-making with the 'Heavenly Host'. There are instances in scripture where God invites the 'Divine Council' to participate in the making of decisions on earthly matters. One of these instances is when they decided how the ungodly Jewish King Ahab was to be brought down (2 Kings 22:20-22):

If we also consider the book of Job, God has discussions with the Divine Council 'Sons of God', based on rewarding those who do good. This epic account unfolds, as the adversary (a former member of the Divine Council) questioned God's omniscience. This was something God was perfectly willing to defend with a whole array of divine assembly watching the events unfold on earth. In the last chapter God is proven right for putting his trust in Job. The book of Job next to Genesis is considered to be one of the oldest books of the Bible (Job 1:6-22).

As the term 'Divine Council' suggests, meetings take place in a 'heavenly council' with the exchange of suggestions and ideas and a final decision takes place to grant permission for a certain method of approach. The appreciation of shared decision-making, however, is unlikely to include the entities entitled the 'Sons of God'. We can also see God's desire for shared rule in the Garden of Eden, when God gives Adam responsibility to subdue the earth and look after it, but as with some of the angelic host, men rebelled and did what was right in their own eyes in a fallen state.

The introduction of Babylon was a prime example of man's rebellion towards God's command to disperse and to be fruitful and multiply. Man built a tower called 'Babel' as an idol of worship to themselves and other spiritual beings. Babel was an elevated platform where humans worshipped a deity. This was the origin of Babylon (Babel). When Moses and Isaiah recalled the origin of this city and tower, they saw more than just man revolting repeatedly against God's commands, but they also saw a spiritual rebellion among the 'Heavenly Host'. This spiritual rebellion can be characterized as members of the 'Divine Council' who didn't want to submit to the throne room of God, neither represent Him in His Kingdom matters, but wanted their own autonomy. They wanted to be just like God, so they rebelled. This characterizes the third fall (Deut 32). They did this by convincing humans to worship them instead of 'Yahweh Elohim'. These created beings thus took the place of God on elevated platforms. The existence of Babylon and the apocalyptic metaphor of the name thus becomes the combined image of rebellion towards God in the heavens and on the earth. After God confuses the language of the people, building stops and God topples the tower. He scatters them to the corners of the earth and then came the formation of Nations. The Book of Deuteronomy is key in communicating how God scattered the former members of the divine council with the humans to the same set locations (Deut 32:7-8). God passes judgement on these entities for their disobedience.

I said, "You are gods,

sons of the Most High, all of you;
[7] nevertheless, like men you shall die,
and fall like any prince."[a] **Psalm 82:6-7**

The nations were thus divided unto spiritual rulers as leaders of geographic locations. The chaos, injustices and overall corruption that is observed in these accounts of those nations are highlighted by the Biblical authors as a two-dimensional phenomenon. Not just a physical one, but also a spiritual realm that is part and parcel of these deeds with shared responsibility. These spiritual entities wanted to be worshipped as idols in the form of debauchery, money and displays of might. Very much like the world we see today, when those in authority give themselves over to the flesh and the spiritual beings that hide behind the idols worshipped, chaos manifests itself.

A good example of this principle in operation is the account of Moses and the Israelites as they exit Egypt and God punishes 10 of the gods belonging to the biggest superpower at the time. Initially the death of all the Hebrew boys were not just orchestrated by Pharaoh himself, but also inspired by the gods of Egypt (Exodus 12:12-13). This prompted God to bring Egypt to justice, including Pharaoh and his gods. Each plague God put upon the Egyptians was a god the Egyptians worshipped. It was not just a slap in the face to their worship of these entities but a never-ending reminder in history that Yahweh is the God of all and that there is none beside him. It was in this process of the rule of these gods being destroyed that God takes a remnant of humanity again and calls them his own. He introduces a third covenant with man through the leadership of Moses and puts in motion another way to view the world and behave. As of course with the Noahide covenant and the Abrahamic covenant, man even under the leadership of Moses lacks the moral responsibility to uphold the covenant with God and they return to the gods of Egypt, Babylon and other entities.

The Hebrews return to slavery being dragged off and exiled in Babylon. They become subjects again to another nation and the spiritual rulers and entities overseeing this empire. They await patiently under many trials and persecutions, their long-awaited return to the promised land. It is in the land of Israel that we are introduced to Jesus. The very incarnation of God who lived amongst us as a man. Jesus was here to save the world and take it back from these rebels. Here again we see this duality of human and spiritual rebels at work, putting their plans in place in unison. Jesus addresses this concept as one and the same, not merely human rebellion and disobedience. We see the plot unfold in an overlapping of the natural and spiritual realm. When Jesus arrived in Jerusalem he was announcing this very fact that, all the prophecies of the Old Testament were coming to pass and that spiritual authorities were being disarmed in a display of both ultimate strength and meekness. The largest exodus was about to take place, freeing humanity from the control of the spiritual rulers of darkness. This was accomplished by his sin offering on the cross, God, giving himself as a ransom for many (Mark 10:45).

Jesus defeated the powers of darkness, by allowing them a grim time of complete control as they unleashed their hate, violence and verbal poison. For the purpose of the whole of humanity Jesus countered this grim appearance of a battle initially seen as lost with the strength of his love and the power of his resurrection life. Following this event, he was able to announce to his own that all power and authority had been given to him. Through the process of the incarnation (putting on flesh), God was the ultimate human and divine partner. This was indeed what the Gospel was all about. The good news and power unto salvation. This is why the disciples shared their faith to a people who understood more fully this duality between humanity and the divine and that indeed Jesus was the risen Christ (ultimate spiritual being) whom they should follow. This person who showed himself in the flesh and who was truly divine would also model a way to be truly human and provide the example of how to practise spirituality in the true essence of freedom.

The victory was won by Jesus and He disarmed them (Colossians 2:15). They were, however, not completely done away with. These spiritual forces still exist and cause just as much trouble as they ever did before; just no longer with a legal right over humanity. They are the root cause of a corrupt world. This is why we are required to love our neighbor and be forgiving to those who persecute us and mistreat us. Our enemy is therefore not other humans, but the spiritual entities that seek to destroy us. These spiritual authorities don't just stand behind idols of wood, stone and iron, but inhabit the very cultural idols we have that inspire one man to war against another, whether in reasoning, or outright division and violence. So, if we are perceptive in recognizing this age old account of history repeating itself again and again, we can pin point the fallen element of the 'Divine Council' at work, perpetuating the rebellion they started at the beginning of the age. This enemy is old, wise, calculated and has developed its strategies over the years, fine-tuning them to the weaknesses of man which is why we are reminded to put on the full armor of God (Eph 6:10-20).

When looking at spiritual beings, the key word 'angel', is clearly too simplistic, as we also have other spiritual beings eg: cherubim and seraphim. Systematically reviewing scripture and looking at the terms referring to the 'Heavenly Host' merely as 'angels', gives us a very incomplete picture. This is a term used to classify most things in the unseen realm, but this does not foster the understanding Hebrews would have had about the spiritual world. A lot of the important vocabulary linked to linguistics was lost over time and gentiles were generally ignorant of the Old Testament theologies regarding the 'Heavenly Host'.

The term 'angel', comes from the Hebrew word 'mal'ak', meaning 'messenger'. Humans can also have that job description sending messages back and forth (Gen 32:3, 7; Deut 2:26; Neh 6:3; 2 Samuel 11:9). This is a term that describes function, whether a spiritual being or not. Dr Heiser points out, that the terms that describe function can be attributed to 'Angel', 'Minister', 'Watcher', 'Host', 'Mediator, 'Cherubim', 'Seraphim'. These terms serve as job descriptions or attributes relating to some task (Heiser 2018).

There are many functions of the heavenly host, some of which are attributed to Cherubim. There are, however, so many misconceptions about this term due to mythology. For centuries for the purpose of the study of angelology we have relied on Greek mythology present in our religious paintings, mosaics, tapestries and stain glass windows. No theologians complained when artists would link Christianity and terms found in it to the cultural myths and appearances of spiritual beings recorded by the ancients in Greek legends. A Cherub is not a fat baby with wings. This is the imagery we need to start moving away from. Cherubim are daunting and imposing figures. If we look at scripture, we see them described as a number of creatures in one, almost in the form of a hybrid spiritual being. Their appearance is never constant and they shift physical traits depending on which account we read. They stand guard between the spiritual and natural realm guarding heaven. If you were to come across a Cherub, you would know that you are about to enter the presence of the Most High. The first time we see Cherubim, is when they are guarding the entrance to the Garden of Eden following the fall of man (Genesis 3:24). The Garden of Eden was sacred space, considered to be Holy, a place where the now disobedient Adam and Eve are no longer welcome to enter.

The Biblical account is, however, not a prolonged exclusion, but God inviting man to be part of fellowship with him again. This is why he gave the Israelites a miniature version of Eden to carry around with them in the wilderness in the form of the 'Tabernacle', followed by a fixed dwelling place for God on the

Temple Mount in Jerusalem. This is significant as in both the sacred space of the 'Tabernacle', and 'Temple', we see the appearance of Cherubim engraved and formed as statues. This served as a reminder to those officiating at the altar that they were indeed in the presence of God. Cherubim are thus always in connection with 'sacred space'. Once a year the High Priest after all the cleansing procedures would enter a place in the Temple called the 'Holy of Holies'. There he would come across this sacred box called the 'Arc of the Covenant'. Formed in one piece upon the box were two golden Cherubim. This formed the footstool of God's throne, which the Cherubim were carrying (Psalm 99). The reason why there was no representation of a throne, was because God was never supposed to be represented in any type of physical image.

The Throne of God, however, only became visible, when the prophets had visions of God sitting on his throne, such as Isaiah. There has been much debate as to the physical representation of these spiritual beings to whether scripture is an anatomy lesson as to their physical attributes in literalism, or if the appearance of the cherubim in the visions were meant to be metaphorical to aid the understanding of the human beholding the scene. Cherubim are described as having 4 wings, whereas Seraphim have 6, but are these physical attributes relevant in Isaiah's vision (Isaiah 6:1-7)? Isaiah's vision of the throne of God and the Cherubim guarding its sacred space represents these beings in a number of forms promoting the majesty and glory of God's creation. To add to the confusion of classifications of heavenly beings, here they are referred to as Seraphim and scripturally speaking, in role and function, there is very little to tell them apart. An interesting point to note is that the term 'Seraphim' actually means 'snake' in Hebrew. A matter of fact, most scholars believe Cherubim and Seraphim are one and the same type of spiritual beings (Sproul 2011).

Isaiah depicts seraphim as a heavenly choir giving praise to their maker as a prime responsibility. The representation of these animal figures (especially cherubim) with wings are a manifestation of creatures with strength. Not just the face of a man, but also bulls, lions and eagles, so even their presence alone lets one know that one is in the presence of might, power and majesty. Technically, these are not really angels. They are 'throne guardians' and as mentioned before, guard sacred space to prevent the defilement of anything or anyone unholy. God's glory and holiness is thus worth protecting. The burning coal placed upon Isaiah's lips by the seraph was a cleansing procedure performed as an act of guarding God's holiness. In the case of the ancient superpower of Egypt, it was the seraphim (cobras) that were used as the throne guardians, protecting the majesty of the Pharaoh. There is no example of either cherubim or seraphim appearing to man on earth to deliver a message (malach) or to assist humans on earth with a task. They are purely spiritual beings that guard sacred space.

Angels in contrast are messengers of God that work on His behalf and their purpose is to minister to those on earth (malach). If we address the issue of the mythology of angels, we do not have any evidence biblically that they have wings. A matter of fact, they look like us, just more daunting sometimes. As humans we do not have physical access to the throne room of God, so God uses these messengers to reach out to us. We see a number of events when angels appear to key characters in scripture: for example the annunciation (Luke 1:26-33). The job description of angels is not merely delivering messages to the people of God, but also to accomplish missions. An example of an angel intervening in the natural realm is when Peter was released from prison (Acts 12:6-11).

There exists a clear ranking system in angelology. The Bible, however, does not give us a clear structure of a middle or lower management system. You have very powerful angels like Gabriel meaning 'God is my power', and Michael 'Who is like God?'. The important learning point as to prevent any kind of worship of these 'Heavenly Hosts' is the meaning of their names themselves. Both Gabriel's name and the name of Michael do not point to the majesty of the spiritual being, but to the glory of God himself. As humans who are created in the image and likeness of God, angels are thus images of both his presence and his power (Dr Mackie 2019). This is how the 'Sons of God', fell as reported in Deuteronomy 32, because these overseers sought glory for themselves, thereby sentencing their lives to everlasting separation from God.

We are not encouraged to look for angels. If they have a mission or are given a message for the people of God, they find us. Needless to say, the supportive role they play is to re-establish the Kingdom of God on earth and to help fulfill God's plan. Angels are therefore used to show the way and serve the people of God. Most of the time, one isn't even going to know about their presence, neither their supernatural intervention in the natural realm.

There are two overlapping realms. The natural and the spiritual, recognizing the difference between the heavens and the earth, both active in each other. To make things simpler, it can be defined as the space we inhabit and the space spiritual beings inhabit. Our realm seems to be pretty standard. However, sometimes the heavenly realm can manifest itself on earth with this overlap. This is evident in many accounts in scripture.

When heaven manifests itself on earth, we have the appearance of someone completely amazing: 'The Angel of the Lord'. We have had a brief introduction to angels, who are messengers from God performing assigned missions, but the 'Angel of the Lord', is clearly no low-level elohim or spiritual being. When we have reference to 'the Angel of the Lord', we are forced to think deeper as to the full nature of the entity at hand, as the personal pronouns communicate far more than the appearance of an angel, but rather Yahweh himself. We can see this in the example of Hagar (Genesis 16:6-16). The Angel of Yahweh is calling to Hagar, but then equally the language moves on to personal pronouns, 'I will multiply your offspring'. Hagar's response is also very telling as she exclaims 'You are the God of the seeing'. The only conclusion we can make from this example is that the Angel of the Lord is clearly Yahweh. This can indeed be puzzling, as scripture is clear that you cannot look upon God and live. The crossing over between 'Angel of the Lord' and 'Yahweh' communicates some type of dualism. God is indeed not within our realm of grasp, but this does not mean that he doesn't reveal himself to mankind in ways that foster understanding in the physical realm. The 'Angel of the Lord' is thus a description in the Bible whereby Yahweh himself intervenes in the world and becomes visible to common man. He is therefore Yahweh, but separate from Yahweh, manifesting himself to us. Throughout the Bible we see glimpses of 'sacred space' experienced in visions by Daniel, Ezekiel and Isaiah. These prophets all see and experience an unimaginable person, full of power and glory who sits on a throne and His name is Yahweh. This is indeed the same person as manifest in the world referred to as 'Angel of the Lord'.

The Bible communicates this theology quite clearly in the account of Moses and the Burning Bush (Exodus 3:1-4). This mysterious figure is at first referred to as 'The Angel of the Lord', then, 'The Lord' and lastly 'God'. Further down the line after the Exodus has taken place, Moses discovers that the person originally in the burning bush is the same individual leading them out into the wilderness in the form of a cloud by day and a pillar of fire by night. This is the same almighty entity who resides in the tabernacle, that travelled with them and later resided in the temple that stood in Jerusalem. The tabernacle formed sacred space as a literal throne room for God. The 'Angel of the Lord' is the Holy personage of God appearing in many respects like a human. It is quite clear where we can be going from here when equating God and man together as one, as this points toward Jesus and the incarnation. This is made very clear to us in the 1ˢᵗ Chapter of John's Gospel as we are told that Jesus existed for all eternity and that He was with God and was God (John 1:1-5).

The incarnation shows us the perfect example that Jesus was distinct from God, but also was God. This in itself was a similar anomaly we discovered between the 'Angel of the Lord' and 'Yahweh'. This was the same presence of the God in the Temple living amongst man. Jesus kept His Glory hidden from man and showed his divine nature only through miracles. An exception to this rule, was when he gave them a glimpse of his true personage during the transfiguration (Mat 17:1-3).

The Old Testament shows us 'The Angel of the Lord', who appears to a certain extent like a man and the New Testament through the incarnation shows Jesus as fully God and fully man. The title of 'The Angel of the Lord', is not used in the New Testament. This was done to avoid the notion or conception that Jesus was limited to an angel, not allowing any chance of downgrading his divinity. To the writers of the New Testament it was evident that Jesus was Yahweh, fully manifested in the flesh, to fulfil the mission of reconciling man to God, forever reuniting both the realms of heaven and earth.

Our contrasting figure in angelology is the 'SATAN', meaning 'the adversary'. The first time we see this character emerge is in the garden of Eden in the first chapters of Genesis. There is no build-up in context to where the 'Satan' came from: this is why in Jewish tradition the serpent is recognized only as a creature and not as Satan, because the complete back story was not available. A matter of fact, Judaism has no recognition of Satan as an influential figure. They attribute good and bad as coming from humans themselves starting with Adam and Eve. Even in the book of Job, Orthodox Jews view Satan as an angel who accuses a person before God at judgement day as a formality, but the general consensus is that God has it covered.

Clearly, however, with all scripture and looking at the whole journey of Biblical accounts in both covenants we can pinpoint the 'Satan' as the shape shifting figure in the Garden. In Genesis 1 God creates a perfect, ordered reality out of chaos and disorder, which is teaming and flourishing with life. Humans are placed in the garden to rule and have dominion over it. They act as his stewards and representatives on earth. Genesis 3 can be viewed and interpreted as not just a rebellion story by humans, but also by the serpent, as this is where the 'Satan' is introduced to the scene.

The serpent was known to be crafty, smart, shrewd and perceptive, possibly indicating a being with a lot of wisdom. This creature is, therefore, clearly set apart as different from the rest of the creatures in the garden and points towards experience and hidden knowledge. Seemingly blessed more than other creatures, but following the 'fall' cursed among all the creatures of the field in an inversion of what once was, to crawl on its belly for the rest of its days in the dust. The adversary stood in a state of rebellion towards the Creator. At this point in this epic we are not yet informed on why he rebelled. He was reportedly intent on ruining every part of God's project and everything that was good. He forms the first portrait of evil in scripture. God created the good out of chaos and created structure. This mysterious figure comes along and attempts to tumble it back into chaos and darkness. Humanity joins the rebellion which brings about chaos and ultimately death. This is where we have this sense of intertwined rebellion in humanity and the spiritual realm. It is a never-ending pattern that we see emerge repeatedly throughout the Biblical text.

Tradition has attributed this serpent figure to be a creature in disguise, perhaps one of the Cherubim. As I pointed out previously, Seraphim means 'snake', and Isaiah 6 lists these Cherubim as Seraphim. This may indeed be an indication in this wider analysis of scripture that this Cherub is a former member of God's throne room. Ezekiel also understood this individual to be a spiritual entity who went rogue and refused to serve under God's wisdom and authority. This entity wanted to be God or at least His equal, which is the same temptation he puts forward to Adam and Eve. He convinced them that they could have dominion over the world, but on their own terms. This also resulted in them being kicked out of the garden just like Lucifer being cast from heaven. From that moment on he slithered away and started working behind the scenes, orchestrating division between humanity.

The adversary has many descriptions from serpent, to leviathan, or even the king of death. Titles like, tempter, father of lies, prince of the power of the air, evil one, or the Greek word Devil 'slanderer', gives us an indication of his function and the way he operates (Zechariah 3). Beelzebub meaning 'Lord of the Flies', conjures up the image of a defiler of everything that is good. 'The Satan' is not a name, it is a role of antithesis. He is in fact anti everything and seeks to undo structure back into chaos and darkness.

The language in scripture upon closer analysis indicates a good figure, going rogue. Amongst all of creation, it would not be unusual to have all God's creatures present during creation, even the Cherubim who later on block the entrance to the Garden of Eden after the fall takes place. This place was sacred space and since God walked and talked with Adam, it may also have been a place in view of the heavenly throne. The account in Genesis portrays 'The Satan', as a fallen figure, just in the same way Adam and Eve are going to be. Every time we have the Hebrew word 'seraph', in the Bible it has a literal meaning of snake. There are 8 examples of this in scripture. It has been theorized that the word can also mean 'burning ones' (Heiser 2018), but we do not have any examples of any type of creature on fire, neither a rich history of Bible commentary making it so. The comparison with Cherubim is evident, as they can look like bulls, eagles, lions and upon closer analysis of the Hebrew like 'snakes'.

The interesting thing in Isaiah 14, is when he talks about the ruler of Babylon, who was a king also trying to make his throne ascend above God's realm (Isaiah 14:12-14). He is linking directly into the Genesis 3 account as a form or parody or parallel with the adversary. This communicated that the serpent was a heavenly being that disguised itself and deceived the humans. An example of an attempted coup and tempting the humans to follow the same path. Isaiah therefore is very intentional the way he brings the seraphim into the account (14 vs 19) 'trampled underfoot', modelled after the Genesis 3 fall.

In Ezekiel 28:11-19 we have a clear description of something that goes beyond a lament of the King of Tyre, also in the form of another parody. We have no evidence of the King of Tyre having been in Eden, or that he was an 'anointed cherub who covers', neither residing on the 'holy mountain of God', which speaks of sacred space. This parody is therefore a dual prophecy, thus comparing the pride of the King of Tyre with the pride of the adversary. It could also be theorized that the King himself was possessed by the evil one, making a link between the physical and spiritual realm. Rather than recognizing the sovereignty of God, this king attributed his riches to his own wisdom and power. He was not satisfied with what he had been given and wanted more, resulting in Tyre taking advantage of the surrounding nations and expanding its own wealth at the expense of others. In the same way Satan's pride led to his fall and will eventually lead to his final destruction. The prophecy against the city of Tyre was fulfilled in part by the invasion of Nebuchadnezzar (Ezekiel 29:17-21) and brought to its final destruction by the Greeks (Alexander the Great). (Lutzer, 2015)

'The Satan', never receives an actual name. He is, however, endowed with descriptions communicating his function, and a venomous snake is one of them. When unpacking the descriptions of the evil one, 'Satan' seems to be the most popular. We see references of images, titles and descriptions of function, but this biblical character is never named. This encourages us to view this figure as a collage of awful deeds, the antithesis of everything that God calls good with the one desire of plunging everything back into chaos. As with the Cherubim and Seraphim, this figure is stooped in mystery. It is the apostle John in the apocalyptic book of Revelation who brings a lot of the imagery we associate with the adversary together into one unified text. He mentions a 'great dragon' an 'old serpent', the 'devil' and 'Satan' all of which we have already seen in different places in scripture. The apostle John brings a lot of clarity as to this elusive character being talked about. John knits all these key descriptions and nouns together to avoid any type of confusion as to who is being referred to, serving as a great summary in the last book of the Bible of this character. This entity is the ruler of everything that is fallen.

Lower-level evil entities come into play when we take another look at the 'Divine Council'. In the Torah we discover that many of these staff members rebelled as well, and the term 'Sons of God', is attributed to these rebellious entities. We have this rather uncomfortable account in Genesis 6, when members of the Divine council 'Sons of God', had been given a role to perform on earth to oversee certain areas. They saw that the daughters of men were fair and decided to leave their abode and mate with women, causing offspring that were known to be Giants and men of renown (Genesis 6 1-4 ESV).

These beings were known as the Nephilim. There are naturally many characters in the Bible that bring about a certain level of awe and fascination, but by far, these come across as the most strange and disturbing. Strange to us, but the ancients who wrote this information down and recorded it in history, plus the people who read it, did not have a problem in viewing it as accurate. These scary beings make an appearance in a lot of accounts in the Biblical narratives. Even historians after the second temple period record such beings: This would seem highly unlikely if we were to view the spirit world and the physical world as unrelated separate realms, but there exists this overlap and the Bible accounts do teach us that spiritual beings do enter the physical realm, even if to sit down and eat (Abraham and the three visitors Gen: 18). In the account of Sodom and Gomorrah we see this overlap between the physical and spiritual again in Genesis 19, as the inhabitants take a shine sexually to the two 'Hosts of Heaven' who came to save Lot and his family before destroying the city.

This overlap between spiritual beings and physical requirements potentially being fulfilled, blurs the lines of normal understanding. In the Old Testament, whenever you have the reference of 'Sons of God', you know scripture is talking about spiritual beings, including 'Hosts of Heaven'. The events of Genesis 6 are confirmed by Jude (Jude 5-7) who wrote the epistle of Jude. He links these accounts of the 'Sons of God', with Sodom and Gomorrah. Jude speaks of disobedient Angels that did not keep their abode, not keeping their proper domain. He informs us that these entities are kept in eternal bonds in a place of darkness awaiting judgement. He is linking Genesis 6 with 19.

This was Jude's understanding of these accounts including all the others in the faith during his day, archived in the dead sea scrolls. Josephus also recorded these events in 'Antiquities of the Jews', chapter 3. The Apostle Peter without question refers to these same accounts and links them. No doubt Peter was fully aware what was written in some of the second temple literature:

⁴For if God did not spare angels when they sinned, but cast them into hell[a] and committed them to chains[b] of gloomy darkness to be kept until the judgment; ⁵ **2 Peter 2:4-5**

The book of Enoch which counts as Second Temple literature

was well understood by Jews during the intertestamental period and records the accounts from Genesis 6 in similar, albeit more detail in Enoch Chapter 7. The book of Giants also follows the similar scripting.

So there exists this whole tradition of giant demi-gods who are mighty men and kings of epic proportions. King David and his strong men wiped out the last remnant of them. Every child who has been to Sunday school knows of the account of David slaying Goliath. If we consider the Dead Sea Scrolls, including the book of 'Enoch', 'Jubilees', 'The wisdom of Ben Sira', and Jude, we cannot escape the disturbing fact that Genesis 6 was not just an inference of a deed, it was factually laying down for us as something that happened between 'The Sons of God', and human women resulting in this terrible offspring. Other interpretations of scripture only developed through later traditions of the Church, as biblical accounts were no longer viewed through the lens of Judaism. Catholicism, the Great Schism and the Reformation, were completely at odds with the actual world view in its original context.. Augustine and Jerome did not hold to the Enochian context of Genesis 6: however, Ireneaus and Clemente did. Later theologies excused Genesis 6 as a commentary based on the Godly lineage of Seth mixing with the ungodly lineage of Cain. Scripture does not encourage this as genealogies are recorded with great detail to avoid misconceptions, so this theory is simply used to explain away something which comes across as very uncomfortable

Surrounding Israel were ancient Kingdoms that were protected by these enormous warrior kings who in themselves were part human, part 'Sons of God', and possessed divine wisdom beyond that of normal mortal man. The authors of scripture, however, do not encourage these beings to be honored, as they were part human rebels captured in darkness. These kings spread unimaginable violence and one of those kings goes on to build the city which we will forever associate with an evil kingdom and that is Babylon in Genesis 10. The builder of this great city was Nimrod and his name is associated with the word 'rebel'. This kingdom is the third large scale rebellion or fall where they build a big tower attempting to make a name for themselves, but God scatters them. It is Moses who brings a lot more context to this situation when he lets us know that it was this particular rebellion that prompted God to hand over the nations to the rebellious 'Hosts of Heaven', the gods of money, sex, power and violence (Deuteronomy 32:8). Moses is the first person to assign the word 'demons' to these heavenly hosts, as they were considered as lesser spiritual beings (Prof. Jonathan Ben. Dov, 2014).

When we view the world and its corruption, we need to know and understand that it is actually these demonic entities that are behind the chaos. They are not just responsible for this widespread chaos in societies, but also on a personal level where they exploit and entice human flesh in greed and selfishness, not just humanity's carnal nature, but also infirmities. Anything that works as the antithesis of God's good creation is attributed to demons and 'The Satan', as they attempt to force creation back into chaos, disorder, darkness and death. This is the main reason Jesus makes it clear that his enemy is not humanity, as he came to save us from the power of the adversary. Jesus knew that it would cost him everything at every level to defeat death itself and that is what he did: furthermore, for that brief time, it cost Him everything.

Demons in Jewish culture could not be cast out: this is why they were so surprised when Jesus was able to do so. There exists no Old Testament example of anyone casting out a demon. However, David was able through anointed music to settle the spirit of King Saul when he was plagued by them (1 Samuel 16:14-16).

So where do demons come from? It was well understood by the ancients, that the origin of demons, was not specifically the 'Watchers' that were assigned geographical locations, neither the entities that fell from heaven. Second temple Judaism understood that demons were disembodied spirits of the Nephilim, the wicked offspring of the 'Sons of God'. To put it simply, these giants were never a part of God's original creation, as they were a product of spiritual beings and humans resulting in human hybrids. When these beings turned on one another and died, their evil spirits had nowhere to go. They did not qualify for Sheol (the realm of the dead) and they were not chained up with the disobedient angels that left their first abode. They were therefore roaming the earth seeking to be re-embodied again, searching for an entry point, whether human or animal. Their nature is as evil as their actions when their bodies were alive on earth (Heiser, Demons, 2020).

Initially this does seem to stray quite far from traditional Christian orthodoxy, but this theory was first put forward to me as a possibility during a lecture decades ago at Bible college. For serious Bible students, Dr Heiser's arguments are based on ancient Semitic and eastern materials. His central argument is the explanation of three divine rebellions against God. Traditional Augustinian orthodoxy only looks at the Fall in the Garden of Eden. Dr Heiser characterizes the first fall as (1) Satan's initial rebellion against God, secondly (2) 'The Sons of God', in Genesis 6 leaving their remit and taking human wives. Finally the third rebellion (3) as the 'Divine Council', being given territorial rule over the nations, but deciding to take the glory for themselves and going rogue (Heiser, Demons, 2020). This three fold framework does explain most of the Bible's spiritual warfare passages and it thus makes that clear distinction between 'the Satan', 'false gods' and 'demons'.

As we have discovered, names are naturally very important and we derive meaning and identity from them. These meanings naturally are very relevant in scripture and open up enormous detail in regard to patriarchs and spiritual beings. It is interesting that the only two specific names mentioned in scripture in regard to angels in the canon of 66 books are:

'Gabriel' and 'Michael'. There is no other record of a specific name of an angel serving God in the protestant canon. We have covered 'The Angel of the Lord', and concluded that this person is Jesus, before the incarnation. Gabriel means 'God is my power', and Michael means 'Who is like God?'. The important learning point as to prevent any kind of worship of these heavenly hosts is the meaning of their names themselves. Both Gabriel's name and the name of Michael do not point to the majesty of the spiritual being, but to the glory of God himself. As humans who are created in the image and likeness of God, angels are thus images of both his presence and his power (Dr Tim Mackie, 2019). This is how the 'Sons of God', fell as reported in Deuteronomy, because these overseers sought glory for themselves thereby sentencing their lives to everlasting separation from God. Yahweh does not provide a process of redemption for rebellious members of his Heavenly Host.

Angelology is a fascinating subject; however, we are not encouraged to look for them. If they have a mission or are given a message for the people of God, they find us! Needless to say, the supportive role they play is to re-establish the Kingdom of God on earth and to help fulfill God's plan. Angels are therefore used to show the way and serve the people of God. Most of the time, one isn't even going to know about their presence, neither their supernatural intervention in the natural realm. This is the very reason why only two of the Angelic Host faithful to God are mentioned specifically by name in the protestant canon. The Catholic canon of 73 books has the addition of Raphael (Meaning: God has healed) (Tobit).

Michael is specifically described as an archangel in scripture. We see him referenced in the books of Daniel 10:13; 21, Jude 1:9 and Revelation 12:7. Michael is always associated as a high-ranking powerful angel who engages in spiritual battles. He is an archangel, deriving from the Greek word 'archangelos', meaning 'chief' or 'ruler'. The Bible suggests there is a ranking system of the angelic host and it is clear that Michael would stand at the top of that. Daniel 10:13 describes Michael as one of the 'Chief Princes', which may indicate that there are other archangels too, but this is inferred instead of being clearly evidential. It is safe to assume that amongst this leadership structure he stands at the top of the Angelic Host. If we look at Jude 1:9, the definite article is used which promotes the singular form, prompting us to believe that he may indeed be the only archangel. In Daniel 10:21, Michael is described as 'your prince', by another angel. This specific angel is talking to Daniel who is Jewish: therefore, Michael is seen as the force overseeing the protection of the Jewish people. This is also confirmed by Daniel 12:1.

It is clear that the fallen angels mentioned in earlier chapters in this book have been assigned territories, taking from the Deuteronomy world view. One of these is named as the 'Prince of Greece', including a 'Prince of Persia'. It was the 'Prince of Persia', preventing the angel delivering the message to Daniel, whereby the archangel Michael intervened. It may be interesting to point out, that it is the empire of Greece that followed the demise of Persia in history. It is clear to see throughout Daniel chapter 10, that the archangel's duty is to engage in spiritual combat. We also see in 1 Thessalonians 4:16-18, that the archangel is involved in the eschatological proceedings of Christ coming back for his church.

In Jude 1:9 we have the very brief account of the archangel Michael contending with the adversary over the body of Moses. We have a distinct impression that Michael is holding off this engagement until the appointed time. It is clear that Michael is operating in the field of his sphere of influence and is cautious as not to overstep the mark, although one may get the impression that he is giving the adversary a heads up with regard to his future. The last references we have of the archangel Michael are in the book of Revelation 12:7. It is traditionally depicted in eschatology as an epic war being fought at the end of time. However, the timeline is not that clear. We have Michael and his angels fighting against 'The Dragon', and this Dragon and his angels are fighting back. 'The Dragon' is defeated and thrown to the earth. The adversary uses all his strength to wage war against the Saints and anyone holding fast to the testimony of Jesus. There are a number of interpretations to this scripture. Some view this as an event depicting the birth of Jesus, or indeed the birth of Israel as a nation and offspring of people of whom Michael is the protector.

The second named angel in scripture as previously mentioned is Gabriel. It is unclear whether he is an archangel or not. He is always associated with bringing an important message from God. We see his first appearance in the book of Daniel 8:16, then in the New Testament he appears to Zechariah in the temple (Luke 1:19) announcing the soon coming birth of John the Baptist and finally the annunciation to the Virgin Mary (Luke 1:31). As far as messages go, he has the top job and clearly delivers the most important ones. Gabriel's first appearance is to the prophet Daniel, and his role is to explain the vision Daniel is trying to grasp (Daniel 8:16). Gabriel's appearance was in the likeness of a man (Daniel 8:15, 9:21).

The wording of swift flight, many interpret as having swooped down with wings, but this is not clear from the text. The 'appearance of a man', or 'the man Gabriel', is likely to rule this out. This appearance of Gabriel was clearly something to behold, as Daniel was not just terrified and fell down before him, but also sick for a number of days after the dramatic encounter (Daniel 8:27). A few chapters on we see another encounter take place as Daniel beholds someone who has the likeness of man, likely to have been Gabriel. As the angel is present to help him understand this next vision the pattern becomes fairly clear (Dan 10:16). In this chapter there are clearly a number of angels present, one of which was Michael who aided the angel in delivering the message, defeating the

'Prince of Persia' and 'Prince of Greece'. This gives us a good glimpse into the spiritual realm as this confirms the wars that go on in the unseen dimensions that overlap with the natural world. Gabriel was dispatched as an immediate reaction to Daniel's prayer (Daniel 10:12), but was delayed by 21 days until receiving help from the archangel Michael.

Gabriel's next appearance we see in the temple to the priest Zechariah who was the soon to be father of John the Baptist. Zechariah was officiating at the altar and Gabriel appeared at the right hand side of the altar of incense, indicating that his prayers had been acknowledged and received (Luke 1:8-25). Zachariah's wife Elizabeth was old and advanced in years and was unable to conceive. This angelic vision and message formed a miracle and clear intervention by God to allow this couple to have a son: furthermore,: someone who would fulfill the prophecy of the coming Elijah who would prepare a way for the Lord. Zechariah was struck speechless until John was 8 days old in keeping with the law of circumcision and the naming of the child.

The next appearance of Gabriel is during the time of Elizabeth's pregnancy. This is the annunciation to the virgin Mary of the incarnation and birth of the Messiah. This unsuspecting woman was called blessed and highly favoured by the Most High and was told that the fruit of her womb was to fulfil the Davidic covenant (Luke 1:26-38). It is interesting to note, that Mary received the message with faith, being overshadowed by the Holy Spirit and thereby conceiving the Saviour. Zechariah was struck dumb due to a lack of faith and human reasoning: however, then carried out the instructions by faith and Elizabeth conceived. In all three specific accounts that mention Gabriel, we have an awe inspiring being, yet an encounter that brings comfort and joy. Gabriel is clearly a highly ranked and trusted angel, who stands in the presence of God and delivers vitally important messages to those who are willing to be used by Him (Sproul 2011).

When we delve into second temple literature, it is the book of Enoch that gives us far more information in regard to named angels and further context to the Genesis 6 account. The first question people may ask about the book of Enoch however, is linked to the listed Canon. It is not considered part of the inspired 66 books in the protestant Bible, neither part of the Catholic Bible of 73 books, so why is it still considered important to many Christians? 1ˢᵗ Enoch predates the Christian era and has a lot to teach us. Academia refers to this literature as Second Temple Judaism which is the era in between the Old Testament and New Testament, otherwise also known as the intertestamental period. The book of Enoch is relevant, because the New Testament writers would have been fully aware of the content of the book of Enoch, thereby, likely to have influenced their writing.

The Jews would have looked at the Hebrew Bible as the inspired word of God, but also wrote loads of commentary on it, attempting to link accounts in scripture to establish connections and meanings (Lumpkin 2011). This second temple literature including Enoch thus becomes visible in the New Testament as it warranted vast discussions in the early church. This does not mean that Enoch is officially inspired and should be part of the canon, but equally this does not diminish its relevance in view of the prominence shown to it by the Jews of that era. It may be interesting to point out, that it is very well worth reading the same material that Biblical writers read for the purpose of understanding the context of the time. Questions need to be asked as to where the Biblical writer's content comes from, what their goal was in communicating certain issues on specific topics, which in turn makes us more literate readers of scripture. Of course, in view of the aim of this book, it does have a lot of relevance to angelology, as far more names of spiritual beings are mentioned, not just Michael and Gabriel.

The book of Enoch does get a lot of attention, as there were those in the early church who did really feel that it should have been part of the canon. It did not become part of the canon, as it can't just be linked to a historical prophetic figure of the Bible, but also the account of the individual must be witnessed in the holy language of Hebrew. When viewing the Dead Sea scrolls, there are no Hebrew examples of the book. There exist some Aramaic fragments of Enoch: furthermore a group called the Qumran sect who held these books as sacred. This sect wrote commentaries on Enoch and other Temple scrolls (Ethiopian Jews today consider the book to be canonical). This lets us know that these books did have an important status in the religious community. Had the book of Enoch been available in Hebrew, it would have received a lot more merit. This, however, did not concern the early church, as the early church largely consisted of Gentiles and the New Testament was written in Greek. A matter of fact, even if we look at the early Church fathers, very few of them could actually read Hebrew. They thus were able to look at 1st Enoch and see striking resemblance in content mirroring the information in the New Testament.

Those who supported the inclusion of Enoch in scripture eventually died out, and the subject was never really effectively resurrected. The majority rejected the book, but still counted it as an important piece of literature. A matter of fact, Irenaeus one of the earliest Church Fathers, actually quotes Enoch in his writings (Schaff 1885). After a period of time Enoch lost popularity and effectively fell out of use. There was no longer a need for people to read their New Testament in light of intertestamental literature: neither was there an important emphasis placed upon it. The important focus points for theological discussions became the questions church fathers faced in their own day, rather than criticisms of books that had not made it into the inspired canon. We are more sensitive today attempting to read scripture in its original context, because we have the means to do so. We are naturally drawn to primary sources that were not available to theologians of the medieval age, and the Dead Sea Scrolls would be among them.

The book of Enoch is pre-Christian, so naturally Jesus is not a point of reference, but it does have messiah figures in these apocalypses. The author(s) addresses eschatology and a very major question, which is why the world is being brought to an end, giving substance to the act of judgement. The rejection of the righteousness of God is a strong theme in this material. Enoch traces that line of thinking partly to the Fall in the Garden, but as you have read earlier on, a large part of the transgressions finds their root cause in the sin of the 'Watchers', otherwise known as high level elohim (spiritual beings) misusing authority given to them by God. This is the contextual account of Genesis 6 in an Enochian version of that event. The Genesis 6 description of the 'Sons of God', has been replaced with the key words 'Watchers'. Those who are meant to watch and not mess things up!

Enoch gives a rationale why the world has become so intensely evil and corrupt, which really helps to explain why God has reached the point to why he regrets that He had created man. Enoch includes the theme of apocalyptic thinking, an explanation of the proliferation of depravity leading to judgement. Enoch is transported to the heavenly throne room of God where he experiences different levels of heaven, with striking similarities to the revelations of John. This experience is enhanced by angelic guides and interpreters clarifying Enoch's experiences. Any literal pieces of work with a strong emphasis on the angelic is often classified by scholars as Enochian, because these elohim feature more heavily in this book than in any other book in the accepted canon. (Dr Michael Heiser, Enoch, 2020)

The most interesting evidence we can find on the validity of Enoch, are the New Testament books that seem to be informed by Enoch and include important themes in their writing. Jude, 2nd Peter and Revelation have clear distinctions of Enochian scripting. Connection points with the Gospels can also be explored and found, not necessarily word for word, but rather in theme. John who authored the book of Revelation borrows heavily from the Old Testament, but no direct quote word for word. John alludes to things by throwing a number of words in a sentence connecting the dots and bringing a lot of questions together. When John is writing, he takes it for granted that the reader knows their Old Testament inside out, so does not need to take up the time to quote directly. It is interesting that the Book of Life does not have any roots in the Old Testament, but rather in second temple literature in the intertestamental period just like Enoch. It comes as no surprise that a lot of John's heavenly imagery can also be found in the book of Enoch. It is the specific content that gives it away, not word for word quotations. The 'Lake of Fire' is in Revelation 19, Matthew 25, but also features in Enoch. It is also fascinating to see references of 'son of man', in Enoch which is Jesus' main description about himself in the Gospels.

When reviewing the topic of the Watchers ('Sons of God') it is the book of 1st Enoch 10:11-13 that described their demise and imprisonment. This can also be linked into the book of Revelation 9:1-10 (Heiser, Demons, 2020), which is theorized by many theologians as a clear parallel. This is an account of the release of these demonic beings upon the earth as a judgement, leading to the end of the world and judgement day itself.

In all Jewish traditions about the events of Genesis 6:1-4 concerning the 'Sons of God', or as Enoch would describe 'the Watchers', the disembodied spirits of the giants (Nephilim) are viewed as demons in the Gospels and as the spiritual beings Jesus encounters when he casts them out. We find that the offending beings 'The Watchers', are sent back to the pit or abyss and imprisoned until the end of days. This eschatological endpoint exists in Jewish tradition itself. In other words, they are in jail. Revelation 9 describes the opening of the abyss and the release of these demonic powers, specifically the ones that were imprisoned. To anyone familiar with intertestamental literature it is frightfully obvious who these beings are that are released upon the earth. The reason why this is such a big deal, is that they speed up the depravity process of human kind and are linked to the authors of idolatry. Many scholars would suggest this as it is an apocalypse, end of days and a precursor to the return of the Messiah and the day of the Lord. Enoch's warnings are not conditional, but rather a warning of what is going to happen, no matter what.

The book of Enoch's relevance is how it informs us on the topic of Angelology. Ephesians chapter 6 specifically throws out some interesting key words of rulers, authorities, cosmic powers and spiritual forces of evil in the heavenly realms. Scholars in the past have all really thrown these classifications into the word: 'demon'. If we specifically look at the word 'rulers', it is used in Enoch and Daniel. This description is also in 1st Corinthians 2 and Enoch deals with it in a broader sense. The book of Daniel is largely influenced by this idea of geographical rulers ie: 'Prince of Persia', lending itself heavily to the world view of Deuteronomy 32 and Psalm 82, whereby the nations were given up to these rulers as a form of judgement, meaning that chaos was sown among the nations (Heiser, The Unseen Realm 329-330). Geographical rulers stood in enmity toward God and instead of serving their purpose as the 'Angelic Host', decided that they enjoyed being worshipped themselves and went rogue.

This is largely where the apostle Paul gets these descriptions. Naturally, just because the apostle Paul may be allegedly borrowing from the Enochian world view, does not necessarily mean, however, that he is suggesting that the book of Enoch should be part of the inspired canon. The reason why the book of Enoch becomes such a point of interest for Angelology, is that it introduces the context of 'The Watchers', to the confusing passages in Genesis 6. The account of the Book of

Enoch will be forever associated with the increased corruption on earth in Genesis 6:1-4, referring to the 'Sons of God' rather than the 'Watchers'. It thus also becomes a very good explanation point to the key question that troubles most believers and non-believers alike, and that is on the origin of good and evil. Many of the references in Enoch serve as a useful way to fill in the gaps to explain the level of depravity man fell into following the first fall in the garden of Eden and the second fall in Genesis 6.

The interesting aspect about this book is that it also uses names of members of the 'Angelic Host' who left their abode and engaged in activities beyond their remit. These names are not limited. There exists an exhaustive list pertaining to those who left their abode and taught the forbidden arts: furthermore, the chief characters who instigated the crime.

The events of this fall are briefly summarized as a number of angels or 'watchers' having been given a task to watch over humanity. As previously described, they begin to desire the women there and by the prompting of their leader Samyaza, take for themselves human wives and completely according to their own volition, instruct men in skills and arts previously unknown to them. They procreate with human women, who give birth to ravaging giants and with their instruction of forbidden knowledge, sow chaos amongst humanity. They taught their new students technologies such as weaponry, cosmetics, mirrors, astrology, sorcery and other dark arts. The parallel with Genesis 6 using the term 'Sons of God', and Enoch using the term 'Watchers', is undeniable. Eventually we see God bring the flood in both Genesis and Enoch to rid the earth of the evil that has been sown and the flesh which has been so corrupted. The book of Enoch names an angel called Uriel who is tasked to instruct Noah to prevent the complete eradication of the human race. The Fallen Watchers from that moment on were bound in a place called the 'Valley of the Earth', which is confirmed by Jude 6. Enoch lists specific leaders among the fallen angels who engaged in sexual union with women of men. Many of these are also listed in other books including the Zohar and the book of Jubilees.

Through the instructions of the 'Watchers' to humanity, people managed to gain knowledge from a virtual cave man existence resulting in the technological brilliance of the building of the pyramids. It may also point us in the right direction as to why God may have felt it necessary to press the reboot button in view of the increased levels of depravity amongst men. It is particularly Azazel who seems to carry a lot of the pressure of blame as he was the one who taught humanity how to make swords and knives, and shields, and breastplates, teaching them about all the metals of the earth and the art of working them including all the workings of vanity (Enoch VIII). The devastation that then followed was witnessed from above by Michael, Gabriel, Suriel and Uriel and Chapter 9 makes it clear that they were not impressed: so much so that they petitioned the Lord as to what action they should take against the rogue angelic host.

Their petition to God was granted and the archangels were given permission to act. In chapter 10 of Enoch 1, God replies in a manner of passing swift judgement against the rogue Watchers. Furthermore, it is evidently clear that redemption is not available to these entities who failed in the responsibility they had been given and used it to their own ends. Although the Watchers seem to repent of their actions their petition for forgiveness is denied. The archangel Raphael is given the responsibility to bind Azazel hand and foot and imprison him until the appointed time of judgement. The archangel Gabriel was tasked with bringing destruction upon the offspring of the watchers so they would turn on one another and thereby destroy each other, even before the arrival of the great flood. The archangel Michael was instructed to inform Semyaza and his followers of his fate: furthermore, watch the destruction of their offspring and then to suffer the same imprisonment until the appointed hour of judgement and eternal torment.

Evidentially, the book of Enoch does not contradict scripture and is useful material on the origin of demons and the Nephilim. It adds further reasoning as to why many of the angels fell from heaven. Furthermore, serves as a useful ancient source to determine extra names of the 'Angelic Host'. When viewing the pressing question of good and evil, it provides a very good explanation as to why it became morally necessary for God to put into motion the flood in Genesis. The added context of the Enochian history also renders another moral explanation as to why God instructed Joshua to wipe out all the tribes in Canaan who were also descendants of Giants (angelic/human hybrids). This was a clear move to wipe out the seed of sin and further source of corruption in the world.

Interestingly enough, many would prefer to reject the book of Enoch as uninspired, but would be perfectly willing to believe someone else's supernatural revelation on T.V and trust it as an inspired word from heaven. People are desperate to listen to anyone's testimony in regard to angels, as the spirit realm is very interesting. The mesmerising topic of angels has been a fixation for many over the ages. Therefore, it comes as no surprise that a number of misconceptions would accompany these objects of fascination. The source of misconceptions for the most part is largely due to a lack of grounding in academia. Many Bible translations do not even require a Christian translator and the generalization of the term can largely be due to linguistics. There has been little time attributed to ancient sources for the purpose of the context of biblical sources or the use of second temple literature to gain an understanding of Jewish thought during the time of the writing of primary sources. A lot of information we have gleaned in angelology has relied on the imagination of artists and their depictions of heavenly beings in mosaics, tapestry, stain glass windows and paintings. Other perceptions we have concerning angels are the never-ending source of the internet where people speak of their spiritual experiences and encounters.

Many people's revelations of angels include the concept of angelic beings with wings. There is absolutely no reference anywhere in scripture pertaining to that claim. The only biblical examples of spiritual beings having wings are in the case of Cherubim and Seraphim, and technically we have discovered through scripture that these are not angels. They are not used to deliver a 'message', (malach). The terminology of Cherubim and Seraphim is fixed in scripture and does not go beyond their function and are thereby not substituted for each other. The role Cherubim and Seraphim play is to guard the throne of God and his holiness. Their function is to keep watch over sacred space, not to fly to earth and instruct humanity on the plan of God. They also do not appear completely in the likeness of a man but are likened to majestic creatures considered to be fierce in the animal kingdom.

When angels appear to humans, they do so repeatedly in human form, which includes both testaments. The terms 'in appearance of a man', are quite telling. Whether this is their actual form has not been revealed to us. New Testament examples make this so obvious, as we are led to believe by the writer of Hebrews that we may have entertained angels without even knowing it. This is in keeping with making sacrifices in life to please God (Hebrews 13:1-2). Another example that shows us that humans are frequently indistinguishable from angels is when the church community was worried about the apostle Peter, as James had already been killed by the sword under the instruction of Herod. Peter was arrested and imprisoned and guarded by four squads of soldiers. Peter was woken by the angel and literally had no idea if he was experiencing a vision or not. All he did know, is that his shackles dropped off him, he was told to put on his sandals and the angel guided him passed the four squads of soldiers. The most interesting part is when the servant girl who recognized the voice of Peter was made fun of by the community and they explained to her that it is likely to have been his angel standing at the door and not Peter. This goes to show that they were used to spiritual beings in human form or likeness of a man dwelling amongst them (Acts 12:6-17).

When we consider evidence from scripture and the appearance of angels, it is clear that the only time they become recognisable from an ordinary human is if their appearance shines like lightning (Matt 28:3), or if they do something which is clearly evidence of God intervening in the natural realm: for example the destruction of the wicked. There are many examples of this in scripture eg: In Exodus the angel of death struck down the firstborn in Egypt *(Exodus 12:29-32)*. In the book of Kings an angel struck down hundreds of Assyrians in their camp *(2 Kings 19:35)* . In the book of Acts, an angel struck down King Herod and he dies of a parasite infection *(Acts 12:23)*.

One important question in relation to angels is the depiction of angels in art work as women. Angels are spirit beings and gender is a biological attribute. Angels are in fact genderless, and do not manifest themselves in scripture in the appearance of a woman. (Sidenote: In Genesis 6 they did, however, leave their first abode and stepped out of their remit, which was detestable to God) They have always been described as men. In the case of Sodom and Gomorrah they were clearly worth a second look.

 Some people try and suggest that Zechariah chapter 5, pertains to women with wings of a stork, lifting up a basket between heaven and earth, but we do not have an indication that these are actually angels. In the book of Zechariah 5:10, when an angel speaks, it uses the masculine form of the verb, not the feminine. The women with baskets were a symbol of the removal of evil from the land and the people of Babylon which is the residing place of all evil (Heiser, 2018).

A messenger is a job description, and taking on physical form in the appearance of a man helps with getting this job done. Most people, especially Daniel and Zechariah, were quite startled, but this adds to the mystery. The other thing we need to consider is that when angels are sent, that they are not always sent in physical form. We discovered that a spirit from the 'Divine Council' was sent to confuse the mouth of the prophets in order to bring an end to the rule of the unrighteous King Ahab (2 Kings 22: 20-22). The spirit that stood before the Lord to volunteer for this method of approach received permission to accomplish the task, but was not embodied ie: The spirit did not appear in physical form, in contrast to the 'watchers', who did the unthinkable in embodied form.

Church tradition seems to have this notion that when the epic war took place in the heavenlies, one third of the angels fell with the adversary, which leaves two thirds of angels with the blessed Trinity to restore God's plan. Unfortunately, we do not have any evidence of this in scripture. We know the adversary fell from heaven, but we have no reference of a third of the 'Angelic Host' following him. Revelation chapters 9 and 10 are very characteristic of this, and stars or luminaries were frequently used to describe angels, but there is no indication as to the number joining the rebellion (Rev 12:9). On the topic of rebellion, there also seems to be this idea that angels themselves are now set in a fixed place of obedience. We do not specifically get this indication from scripture. It is clear from the whole story that unfolds in the Bible that God's 'Holy Ones', are not perfect or beyond falling.

The book of Job gives us more clarity on this issue and forces us to look at the 'Divine Council' as not without error (Job 15:15; 4:17-18). Although the book of Job is traditionally put on the same time line as the book of Genesis, it is clear that these events are well after the initial fall in the garden of Eden. God puts no trust in his holy ones and he charges his angels with error. God is omniscient and is well ahead of the game. Whether they are immortal or eternal naturally rests upon

God's will. They are created beings, so therefore had a beginning and their end rests with the decisions of the Almighty. In view of the Genesis 6 scenario with the added context of second temple literature, the apostle Paul alludes to something very interesting in regard to 1. Male authority 2. Angelic implication, as not to offend the angels with an uncovered head (1 Corinthians 11:10). Some view this verse as Paul hinting at the possibility of history repeating itself, as the angels are always watching. It is likely, however, that this verse is more in line with symbols of marriage and spiritual headship in the home.

Moving on to the afterlife, one of the popular beliefs concerning angels is that they take a person to heaven when they die. One of the most quoted sources of this is naturally the account of the 'Rich man and Lazarus', which was an account taught by Jesus. Many people for some reason decide that it was a parable, but we have no evidence to suggest that Jesus was not giving an example of the actual workings of life after death. In this account, the rich man faces a place of torment and Lazarus is taken to a place called 'Abraham's bosom', characterized as paradise in the afterlife. This is often seen as the good side of Sheol (Luke 16:22).

The image of angels escorting people to heaven is common both in the Bible and second temple literature including the pseudepigrapha. The archangel Michael disputing with the adversary concerning the body of Moses also helps to impress this image in our thinking (Jude 1:9). In the case of Abraham, 'The Testament of Abraham', (20:10-12) tells of the account of the archangel Michael, bearing his precious soul in his hands. If we look at other apocryphal sources such as the 'Testament of Job' we also see this common theme, as Job falls ill. After a number of days of illness, he was able to see those who were coming for his soul. A chariot arrives and he is greeted by the driver and taking his soul as he flies up to the east, whilst the body is prepared for burial (Testament of Job 52: 1-12). There is no reason to suggest that angels are not a part of escorting a soul into the afterlife, as Jesus himself gives us this example in Luke. Therefore, the second temple literature regarding Job and Abraham may have some truth in them (Heiser 2018).

Within some circles of Christianity there has existed this tradition that humans become angels when they die. A human does not become an angel after death. We will in time receive a resurrection body like Christ (1 Cor 15:35-38), but there is no scriptural evidence to suggest that we become 'messengers', or spirits working on behalf of God to intervene in the natural realm. Just because man has a soul and a spirit, does not mean that we become ministering spirits. If this were the case, it would encourage the practice of spiritism in the Church. A matter of fact, we will no longer be a little lower than the angels as far as altitude is concerned (Heb 2:7), but we will indeed rule with Christ if we persist (2 Timothy 2:12). We shall be like Him (1 John 3:2).

Some Christians have evolved in their ideas and foster the belief that we can command angels to do what we want. I have yet to come across any scriptural evidence to suggest this is possible or encouraged. This idea comes from Hebrews 1:13-14. The first thing we need to realize about these verses, is that they are speaking of the supremacy of Christ. The only time believers feature in these verses pertains to those who are to inherit salvation. We may indeed command angels one day, after we have run the race and passed the test in this life, to go into the next. Only then do we become a part of the judging process of angels (1 Corinthians 6:3). To put this verse into context, if we read the whole of chapter 6, the example of judging angels was used to encourage believers to judge correctly, according to God's law when dealing with disputes. Paul was not happy with believers taking trivial cases to secular courts amongst believers. In the same chapter this also pertains to believers one day judging the world.

In this life, although we are to test the spirits, we do not have authority to project them around the place to get what we want (John 4:1-6). This is not Christian practice and is rooted more in the 'new age', taking up contact with one's guardian angel, or unlocking their power. A matter of fact, we are not encouraged to look for angels at all. They are what their name suggests 'messengers' and spiritual beings that work on behalf of God intervening in the natural realm either in word or in deed. Communion with spirits other than the Holy Spirit is expressly forbidden and in many cases is more reminiscent of witchcraft and the need for following a spirit guide. This is the adversary's oldest trick in the book as he was the deceiver in the beginning:

[14] And no wonder, for even Satan disguises himself as an angel of light. [15] So it is no surprise if his servants, also, disguise themselves as servants of righteousness. Their end will correspond to their deeds'. **2 Corinthians 11: 14-15**

Spiritism is not rooted in main stream Christian thinking and is linked to the occult.

In conclusion, if you desperately want to seek an angel, then seek the 'Angel of the Lord', who is no one else than Jesus himself. The 'Angel of the LORD' encamps around those who fear him, and delivers them (Psalm 34:7). If you require the ministry of angels in your life, then there is one safe way to enhance their engagement, and that is in the form of a frequent and faith filled prayer life. The angel Gabriel was immediately dispatched after Daniel prayed (Daniel 9:23). In the case of Peter in Acts, when the church was praying for him, an angel was sent to him to free him from prison. It is evidently clear from scripture, that prayer and being in communion with Jesus enhances angelic intervention. The only revealed names of angels in the most reliable canon are, 'Gabriel' meaning 'God is my power', and Michael meaning 'Who is like God?'. Both these names in their very nature only give glory to God. In our intense study of the 'Angelic Host' in scripture, we have discovered that God has largely put a veil over the workings of the spirit realm for a reason. The subject is fascinating, but if we seek after further knowledge, why not seek the 'ultimate spiritual' being who is God? A sound and scriptural study of angels will point you towards the majesty of the Father.

FINDINGS OF THE SYSTEMATIC REVIEW

<u>Divine Council</u>

- Yahweh Elohim is God.
- Elohim can also mean 'other spiritual beings'.
- Angel means 'messenger' (malach). It is a description of a particular function.
- Angels can be embodied and manifest in physical form, or influence events on earth in disembodied form as spirits (*2 Kings 22: 20-22*)
- Terms used for spiritual beings can also be 'Sons of God', 'Rulers and Authorities', 'Holy Ones', 'Heavenly Ones', 'Host of Heaven', 'Principalities and Powers', 'Divine Council'.
- There are angels of God, and angels that rebelled and remain in a fallen state. (Some former members of the Divine Council).
- The spiritual realm overlaps with the natural realm.
- The ten plagues were a judgement not just on the people of Egypt, but on the gods of Egypt as well.

(Exodus 12:12-13)
- In the New Testament, Jesus was/is the ultimate spiritual being.
- Jesus disarmed all spiritual authorities (Col 2:15).

Angels, Cherubim and Seraphim

- There are many functions of the heavenly host.
- Cherubim are daunting and imposing figures appearing in scripture as human/animal hybrid spiritual beings.
- Cherubim shift traits according to different Biblical accounts.
- Cherubim stand guard between the spiritual and natural realm guarding heaven.
- Cherubim and Seraphim are throne guardians that guard sacred space.
- We only have one Biblical account of Seraphim.
- Seraphim form a heavenly choir in the throne room and guard the holiness of God.
- Seraph can also mean 'serpent,' or 'burning ones'.
- Cherubim are always portrayed as creatures of majesty and strength with faces of humans, bulls, lions and eagles.
- Cherubim and Seraphim are not angels and do not perform functions on earth to deliver messages (malach), or intervene in human affairs.
- Cherubim and Seraphim do have wings.
- Cherubim, Seraphim and the archangel Michael are images of God's presence and power.

The Angel of the Lord

- The 'Angel of the Lord', is a description in the Bible whereby Yahweh himself intervenes in the world and becomes visible to common man.
- The term 'Angel of the Lord', 'The Lord', and 'God' are interchangeable. (Exodus 3:1-4)

- The 'Angel of the Lord' is the Holy personage of God appearing in some respects like a human.
- The 'Angel of the Lord', is the visible pre-incarnate manifestation of Christ to man in the Old Testament.

The Adversary

- The Satan is Hebrew for 'the adversary'.
- The adversary forms the first portrait of evil in scripture.
- Tradition views the adversary as a fallen Cherub.
- The descriptions of the adversary often denote function such as 'tempter','evil one', Devil 'slanderer', Beelzebub 'Lord of the flies', or untrustworthy creatures such as snakes, leviathan or indeed the king of death.
- The adversary seeks to throw everything back into chaos and destruction, literally a pre-creation state.
- 'The Satan', never receives an actul name.The Bible largely avoids the adversary with having an actual name, as this presupposes the honour and dignity of being named.
- In Ezekiel the adversary is called a Cherub and Seraph in Isaiah.
- Church tradition associates Isaiah 14 with Lucifer 'light bearer', in the Vulgate.
- The apostle John is the person who ties many descriptions of the adversary together in one verse, knitting everything together in this unfolding story, bringing clarity to this elusive spiritual being. 'Great Dragon','Old Serpent', called the 'Devil' and 'Satan' (Revelation 12:9).

Demons

- 'Sons of God', are always titles for fallen 'Divine Council members'.
- Second Temple Judaism believed in the Genesis 6 account, whereby spiritual beings had offspring with human women.
- Second Temple Judaism understood that demons were disembodied spirits of the Nephilim, the wicked offspring of the 'Sons of God'.
- This is not just documented in Second Temple writings, but also Josephus who was a Jewish historian employed by Rome.
- After their destruction, the spirits of these angelic/human hybrids had nowhere to go. They did not qualify for Sheol as they were never meant to be created and did not follow their fathers who were locked in chains until judgement. These spirits therefore roam the earth seeking to be re-embodied again, searching for any entry point, whether beast or man.
- Second temple Judaism does not just recognise one Fall, but three divine falls. The first fall as (1) Satan's initial rebellion against God, secondly (2) 'The Sons of God', in Genesis 6 leaving their remit and taking human wives. Finally the third rebellion (3) as the 'divine council', being given territorial rule over the nations, but deciding to take the glory for themselves and going rogue.

Angels named in Scripture

- The only named angels in scripture are Michael and Gabriel in the protestant canon of 66 books
- Gabriel means 'God is my Power'.
- Michael means 'Who is like God'?

- Both names point to the majesty of God, not the spiritual being.
- Michael is specifically referred to as an archangel.
- Michael is a warrior archangel and a chieftain.
- Michael is the force overseeing the Jewish people.
- Michael took on the'Prince of Persia', and 'Prince of Greece', in sprititual combat.
- Michael and his angels were responsible for throwing the Great Dragon out of heaven (Rev 12).
- Gabriel is always associated with bringing the most important messages to earth, whether to Daniel, Zechariah or Mary.
- Gabriel can appear with the likeness of a man, but be quite terrifying in the appearance of light.
- Raphael meaning 'God has healed', is only to be found in the Catholic Bible in the book of Tobit.

The relevance of the book of Enoch

- The book of Enoch 1 is Second Temple Literature.
- The book of Enoch is relevant as the New Testament writers were fully aware of the content of Enoch.
- Enoch is not considered to be the inspired Word of God, but a book does not have to be in the Bible to be theologically relevant.
- The Qumran sect held the book of Enoch as sacred and included it in the Dead Sea Scrolls.
- Had Enoch have been written in Hebrew, it would have warranted more validiy.
- Enoch is an apocalyptic book.
- The fall of the 'Watchers', is the contextual account of Genesis 6 in an Enochian view of that event.
- The books of Jude, 2nd Peter and Revelation have clear distinctions of Enochian scripting.
- Jude mentions Enoch by name.
- The 'Watchers', are linked to the authors of evil.
- Enoch informs us about angelology in detail and lists

many more names of angels and watchers.

- Enoch lends itself heavily to the Deuteronomy 32 and Psalm 82 worldview concerning fallen angels as geographical rulers and principalities.
- Enoch uses the term 'Watchers', instead of 'Sons of God'.
- Enoch is a good source informing us about the origin of evil and the passing on of forbidden knowledge and dark arts.
- There is no instance where the book of Enoch contradicts scripture in the accepted canon.
- The Ethiopian Orthodox Church includes Enoch in their canon.
- The accounts in Enoch serve as a good reason why God had to bring about a global flood to wipe out the corruption of all flesh and why he instructed Joshua to destroy all the tribes in Canaan.

Myths and Misconceptions

- Our knowledge on angelology has largely been reliant on the imagination of artists and their depictions of heavenly beings in mosaics, tapestry, stainglass windows and paintings; not on primary sources or acedemia.
- Angels contrary to popular mythology do not have wings. Cherubim and Seraphim do have wings.
- Angels according to scripture manifest in appearance of men, not as women. There are no examples of angels manifesting in appearance of a woman.
- Humans can in some cases be indistinguishable from angels e.g (Acts 12).
- Peter's angel may not have been unlike Peter in appearance (Acts 12).
- Many have entertained angels unaware (Hebrews 13).
- Angels intervene in the natural world to save human beings from harm and in some cases pass deadly

judgement on the wicked in accordance with the will of God. (Exodus 12:29-32)(2 Kings 19:35)(Acts 12:23).
- When angels manifest, they can do so in the appearance of men, but also shine as bright as lightning, with clothes as white as snow (Matthew 28:3).
- Angels can fulfill their mission as spirits in disembodied form (2 Kings 22:20-22), or accomplish their assignment in embodied form.
- In Genesis 6, the 'Sons of God', left their first abode in embodied form and did the unthinkable.
- There is no evidence in scripture that one third of the angelic host fell with the adversary. This is tradition, but not evidence based.
- Angels have free will and are not beyond falling, and if they sin are beyond redemption.
- There is scriptural evidence to suggest that angels can take people to heaven.
- Humans are human, angels are angels. Humans do not become angels after death. The redeemed have a higher calling.
- The redeemed will share a messianic rule with Jesus.
- Believers have not been given the authority to command their own personal angel to do their bidding. Christians are required to pray to God and He may release angels according to His will and purpose. We are discouraged from taking up communication with spirits in scripture.
- Satan masquerades as an angel of light.
- Had Jesus have commanded Angels to intervene on his behalf, he would not have used the example of asking the Father first (Matthew 26:53).
- A sound study of angels will lead you to the majesty of the Father.

The Angelic Host

BIBLIOGRAPHY

Ben-Dov, Prof. Jonathan & Sanders, Seth , *Ancient Jewish Sciences and the History of Knowledge in Second Temple Literature*, ISAW and New York University Press 2014

Clementine Homilies, Homily VIII, *Chapter XIII.*

Lumpkin, Joseph, The Books of Enoch: The Angels, The Watchers and the Nephilim, 2011

Gangel, Kenneth, Genesis: Holman Old Testament Commentary, B & H Books, 2003

Heiser, Dr Michael, Unseen Realm, Lexham Press, 2015

Heiser, Dr Michael, Angels, What the Bible Really Says about God's Heavenly Host, Lexham Press, 2018

Heiser, Dr Michael, Demons, what the Bible really says about the Powers of Darkness, Lexham Press, 2020

Heiser, Dr Michael, Reversing Hermon : Enoch, the Watchers & the Forgotten Mission of Jesus Christ, Lexham Press, 2020

Heiser, Dr Michael, A Companion to the Book of Enoch: A Reader's Commentary, Vol I: The Book of the Watchers (1 Enoch 1-36) 2020

Irenaeus, Against Heresies, A Discourse in the Demonstration of Apostolic Preaching; 18, 202 AD

Josephus, Flavius, Antiquities of the Jews, Book 1 Chapter 3. Concerning the flood; and after what manner Noah was saved in an ark, with his kindred, and afterwards dwelt in the plain of Shinar.

Lutzer, Erwin W, God's Devil: the Incredible Story of How Satan's Rebellion Serves God's Purposes, Moody Publishers, 2015

Mackie, Dr Tim, Elohim, Bible Project, 2019

Mackie, Dr Tim, Cherubim, Seraphim and Snakes - The Bible Project Q&A 2021

Mackie, Dr Tim, Angels and Cherubim, Bible Project, 2019

Mackie, Dr Tim, Satan, Lúcifer and Isaiah 14, The Bible Project Q&A, 2021

Nickelsburg, George W.E. 1 Enoch : A new translation : based on the Hermeneia commentary. Minneapolis: Fortress Press, 2004

Schaff, Philip, The Apostolic Fathers with Justin Martyr and Irenaeus - Christian Classics Ethereal Library, 1885

Sproul, R.C, Unseen Realities: Heaven, Hell, Angels, and Demons, Christian Focus Paperback, 2011.

AUTHOR'S OTHER WORKS

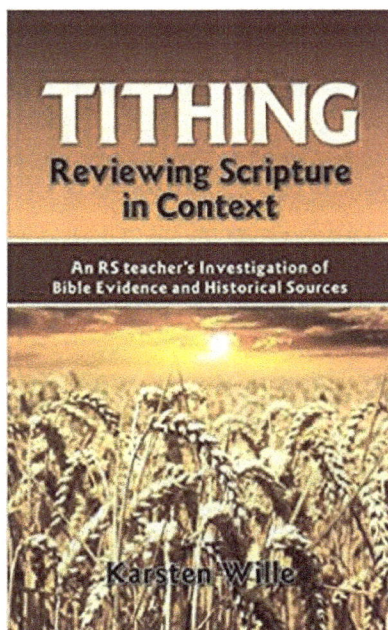

Tithing is mentioned many times in the Bible and many theories have been developed over time especially concerning the need of giving a tenth of one's income in the New Testament Church. This subject has divided many people with a special focus on the Law and freewill giving. It is Karsten's intention to delve into scripture, commenting on the customs and cultures of the times they were written and the audiences they were meant to capture. Scripture is only useful if we rightly divide the word of truth, which is consequently only possible if we study ourselves approved (2 Timothy 2:15). Karsten summarises all the main points of the study of scripture and context, then finalises the findings in easy to navigate bullet points to form an overview, narrowing evidence into a systematic review. A clear picture of the subject arises, whereby you can determine your own conclusions regarding this topic.

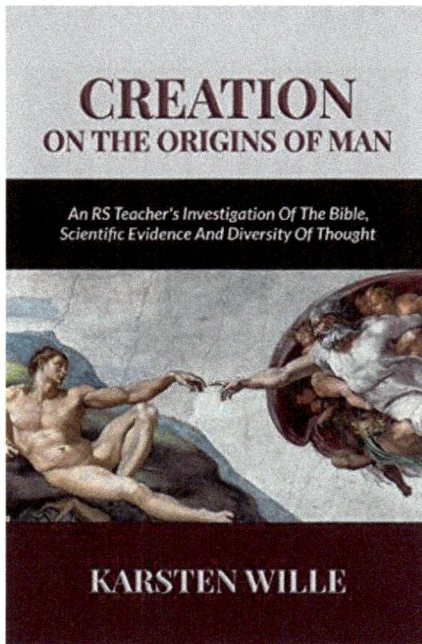

There has never been a published scientific work that has shaped the world into a streamlined view, permeating the way we perceive the physical, biological and psychological sciences today such as Darwin's book 'On the Origins of Species'. His work has not just been confined to these fields, but has influenced both history and Christian Theology as well. The findings of Darwin have been readily accepted as a suitable explanation for the beginning of all life by the Catholic Church and other liturgical denominations. This book seeks to question the validity of Darwin's 'On the Origins of Species', and whether it should be accepted by the Church as a suitable alternative to scripture. This will include the difficult task of discussing philosophy and science as a whole. Karsten summarizes all the main points of the teachings of the church and scientific evidence.

INVESTIGATING THE
BIGGEST QUESTIONS IN
CHRISTIANITY

KARSTEN WILLE

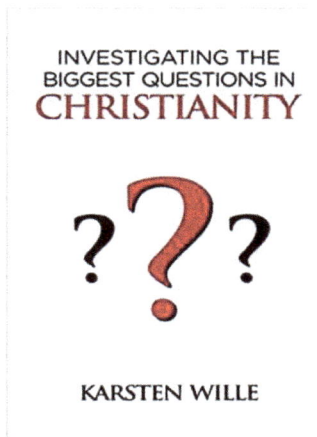

This book aims to analyse scripture in the context of all Bible evidence relating to the most frequently asked questions in Christianity. These top ten topics have divided many in the body of Christ confirmed in various different teachings of the church. Many of the answers to these questions in scripture are clear cut, whereas others need a lot more scrutiny by weighing up all scripture and not just particular chosen verses to come to an informed decision. My intention is not to push for a particular teaching of the church, but rather ask the most important question; what does the text say? Some of the most frequently asked questions in Christianity are philosophical, whereas other questions will be on an ethical and moral basis. When investigating many of the answers to these questions it will be vital to take it from a scriptural standpoint, that the word of God does not change (Hebrews 13.8) (James 1:17) (Mal 3:6). This also means that He has not changed His mind according to the moral guidance He has given us. Any answers to the questions will not rely on subjective evidence based on the way society feels about a given situation, but will be based on the unchanging objective word of God. 'All scripture is given by inspiration of God, and is profitable for doctrine, for reproof, for correction, for instruction in righteousness'. (2 Timothy 3:16)

ABOUT THE AUTHOR

Karsten is an international award-winning author 'Tithing: Reviewing Scripture in context'. He has worked as a Pentecostal Pastor, planting churches in the UK and working in a Missions and Evangelism Department ministering the Gospel in Africa, Asia and South America. With a PGCE from Exeter University and studies with the Open University in Educational Research, he has taught Religious Education in Christianity and Judaism for the last 20 years. He has published 4 books and speaks at Bible academies, various radio programmes and T.V

The Angelic Host

www.ingramcontent.com/pod-product-compliance
Lightning Source LLC
Chambersburg PA
CBHW071754090426
42737CB00012B/1813